DATE DUE

	DATE DUE	
	SEP 3 0 2007	
MAR 1 1 2009	MAR 0 3 2010	
	SEP 1 6 2007	
MAR 1 8 2013	SEP 2 4 2009	
	DEC 11 2012	
	NOV 1 5 2011	

Eyewitness
CRIME &
DETECTION

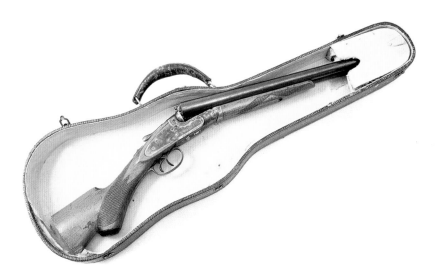

Hungarian
warrant card

Police
cap

British Bow Street
Runner's gun

Drill used
to break into
safe-deposit boxes

Police uniform
used in
Pennsylvania

Alarm system for
detecting theft
from desk drawers

British
peeler's
truncheon

Scene-of-crime
shoe covers

Magnetic
fingerprint
brush

Hand print

Eyewitness
CRIME &
DETECTION

U.S. marshal's badge

British policeman's
helmet badge

Written by
BRIAN LANE

Photographed by
ANDY CRAWFORD

Al Capone's cigarette case

Black Jack Ketchum's
handcuffs

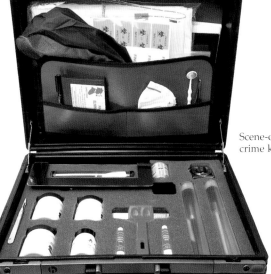

Scene-of-
crime kit

John Dillinger's death mask

British policeman's lamp (1930s)

DK Publishing, Inc.

German police cap

Policeman's rattle

Policewoman's truncheon

Truncheon

British peeler's top hat

DK

LONDON, NEW YORK, MUNICH,
MELBOURNE, and DELHI

Project editor Kitty Blount
Art editor Carlton Hibbert
Senior managing editor Gillian Denton
Senior managing art editor Julia Harris
Production Lisa Moss
Picture research Sean Hunter
DTP designer Nicky Studdart

REVISED EDITION
Editors Barbara Berger, Laura Buller
Editorial assistant John Searcy
Publishing director Beth Sutinis
Senior designer Tai Blanche
Designers Jessica Lasher, Diana Catherines
Photo research Chrissy McIntyre
Art director Dirk Kaufman
DTP designer Milos Orlovic
Production Ivor Parker

This Eyewitness ® Book has been conceived by
Dorling Kindersley Limited and Editions Gallimard.

This edition published in the United States in 2005
by DK Publishing, Inc.
375 Hudson Street, New York, NY 10014

05 06 07 08 09 10 9 8 7 6 5 4 3 2 1

Copyright © 1998 © 2005 Dorling Kindersley Limited

A catalog record for this book is
available from the Library of Congress.

ISBN 0-7566-1386-8 (Hardcover) 0-7566-1395-7 (Library Binding)

Color reproduction by Colourscan, Singapore
Printed in China by Toppan Printing Co.,
(Shenzhen) Ltd.

Discover more at
www.dk.com

California police
cloth badge

British peeler's uniform

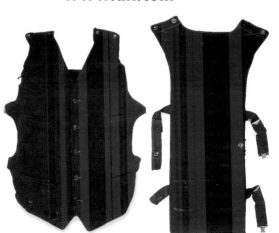

Bonnie Parker's body armor

Contents

8
Crime and society

10
Law and order

12
Justice and sentencing

14
Bounty hunters and thief takers

16
Theft and burglary

18
Swindles and frauds

20
Forgery

22
Murder and kidnapping

24
Prohibition

26
International gangsters

28
Smuggling and piracy

30
Fire!

32
Police uniforms

34
Police agencies

36
Detectives

38
Undercover surveillance

40
Crime scene

42
Following clues

44
Fingerprints and DNA

46
Forensic analysis

48
The bare bones

50
Attention to detail

52
Criminal characteristics

54
Following a scent

56
Outlaws

58
Strange but true

60
Did you know?

62
Timeline

64
Find out more

66
Glossary

72
Index

Prison uniform of the
type worn at Alcatraz

Crime and society

CAIN AND ABEL
According to the biblical book of Genesis, Cain, the elder son of Adam and Eve, was a farmer. He made a sacrifice of corn to God. His younger brother, Abel, a shepherd, offered his best sheep. God accepted the sheep, but rejected the corn. Moved by jealousy and anger, Cain killed his brother. This, says the Bible, was the first murder.

T HERE ARE FEW CORNERS of the world that are free from crime. Crime is defined in the dictionary as "an act punishable by law," so its nature depends on the laws of each society. The laws of a Judeo-Christian society follow the teachings of the Bible; many of the moral values of these societies are derived from the Ten Commandments. An Islamic society adopts the wisdom of the Koran. Among many African and Asian groups, tribal rules of conduct are often decided by a council of elders, who decide both what is a crime and how to punish it. Whatever the basis of their legal system, all societies must deal with people who defy the law.

LOOTING AND BLACK MARKET SALES
Sometimes the results of war are destruction and lawlessness. In this confusion, some people steal goods from damaged houses and shops. This practice is called looting. The term comes from the Hindi word *lut*, which means "booty." Looting also occurs during peacetime – when there are inner-city riots, for example. Closely associated with looting is the secret selling of food and other items that are either scarce or heavily rationed. This is known as selling on the "black market."

EMPEROR JUSTINIAN
Flavius Anicius Sabbaticus Justinianus, called Justinian the Great (483–565), was a Byzantine emperor who laid the foundations of Roman law. Many of the modern world's legal systems are based on this body of law, called the Justinian Code

The Artful Dodger picks a pocket while Oliver looks on in horror in a scene from Charles Dickens's novel Oliver Twist

DRACONIAN LAW
Above is an extract in the original Greek of Draco's *Laws on Murder*. Draco was a lawmaker in Athens, Greece (624–621 B.C.). He ordered execution for all crimes, including laziness. He believed even minor crimes warranted death, and therefore could not find a greater punishment for more serious crimes. The term "Draconian laws" evolved from Draco's harshness

19TH-CENTURY CRIME WAVE
The increasing wealth of factory owners brought about by the Industrial Revolution in Europe widened the gap between rich and poor, and crime grew. This illustration from *Oliver Twist* by Charles Dickens shows some pickpockets in operation. This increase in crime helped lead to the founding of police forces and the strengthening of laws and punishments. In the first quarter of the 19th century, there were 156 crimes punishable by death, including heretical preaching and monopolizing corn.

STORMING THE BASTILLE
The main prison in Paris during the French Revolution was the Bastille. In July 1789, it was stormed by a Parisian crowd and the prisoners were released. The most unusual of these liberated "prisoners" were several hundred books that had been imprisoned for the crime of being critical of the monarchy.

Contemporary print of the blazing Bastille

LAW IN VARIOUS CULTURES
Not all legal systems are based on Roman law. In parts of Africa and Asia, tribal chiefs advised by holy men administer justice. In North Africa, shamans and witch doctors dictate the law.

Lion mask of a shaman belonging to Africa's Ashanti tribe

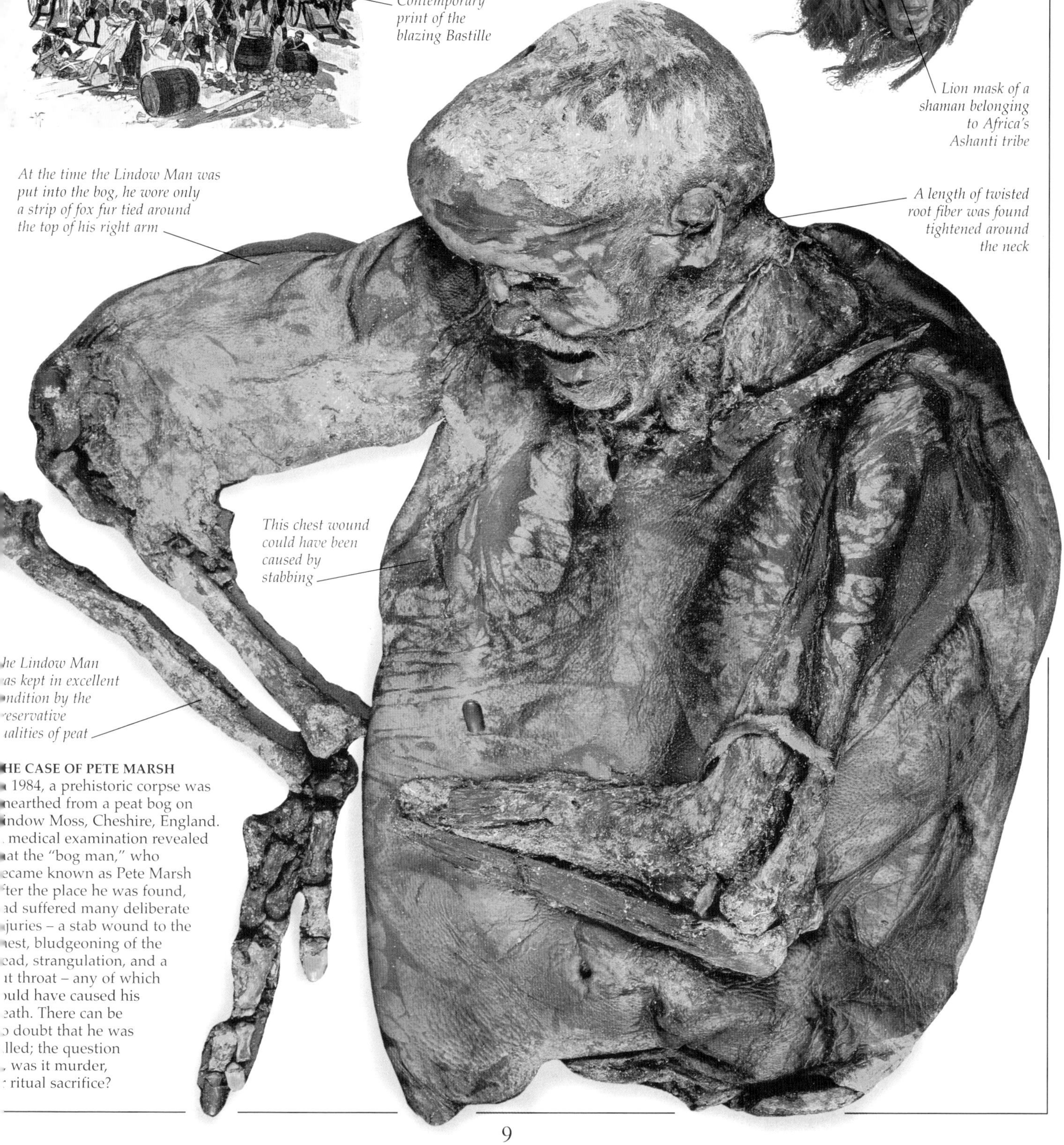

At the time the Lindow Man was put into the bog, he wore only a strip of fox fur tied around the top of his right arm

A length of twisted root fiber was found tightened around the neck

This chest wound could have been caused by stabbing

*he Lindow Man
as kept in excellent
ndition by the
eservative
ualities of peat*

HE CASE OF PETE MARSH
1984, a prehistoric corpse was
earthed from a peat bog on
ndow Moss, Cheshire, England.
medical examination revealed
at the "bog man," who
ecame known as Pete Marsh
ter the place he was found,
ad suffered many deliberate
juries – a stab wound to the
est, bludgeoning of the
ead, strangulation, and a
t throat – any of which
uld have caused his
eath. There can be
doubt that he was
lled; the question
was it murder,
ritual sacrifice?

9

Law and order

SINCE ALL SOCIETIES SUFFER CRIMES, they have all developed systems of law by which to judge wrongdoers and assist the law enforcement officers in bringing criminals to justice (pp. 12–13). Officers try to keep order by preventing people from committing crimes and thereby breaking the law. In many countries, laws fall into two categories, "common" and statutory. "Common" law is based on previous legal judgments and is often unwritten law. Statutory law is a collection of written laws, or statutes, enacted by parliaments, congresses, and legislatures.

Collar prevents garroting, or strangling from behind

Belt to which truncheon and lantern are attached

Lantern with thick, round glass front, like a bull's-eye

Armband worn to show officer is on duty

White, lightweight trousers worn in summer

Bobbys's truncheon, sometimes called a "nut-cracker"

Bobby's hanger (saber) and sheath worn on the belt only on ceremonial occasions

WOODEN RATTLE
A wooden rattle was used to signal an alarm or call for help. Rattles were carried in a pocket of one of the tails of the jacket. Rattles, rather than whistles, were used initially because hotel doormen used whistles to call cabs. By 1880, however, increasing traffic noise made whistles essential.

Double-barreled pistol of 1763 carried by a Bow Street Runner

BOW STREET RUNNERS
In 1750, crime had become such a problem in London that Sir Henry Fielding, the magistrate at Bow Street Court, assembled a force of six men to patrol the streets in and around the city. They were called Bow Street Runners because night and day they were available, within 15 minutes, to "run" after a criminal. Despite growing in numbers and effectiveness, the Runners were disbanded in 1829.

BOBBY'S UNIFORM
Sir Robert Peel was the British home secretary from 1822 to 1830. He founded the Metropolitan Police at Scotland Yard. These officers became known as "peelers" or "bobbies," shortenings of Sir Robert's name. The force was known for its distinguished uniform.

Stovepipe hat, strong enough to protect the head and sturdy enough to stand on and see over a wall

THE FIRST FRENCH POLICE
The Marquis de Louvois (left) and Gabriel La Reynie founded the police force in Paris, France, in 1667. As chief of police, La Reynie abolished the *cour des miracles*. A *cour des miracles* was an area of sanctuary in the center of each French city in which beggars and bandits hid from the law. He also introduced a mounted and a pedestrian police force in Paris.

THIEF AND DETECTIVE
When the infamous French thief François-Eugène Vidocq was released from his last term in prison in 1809, he offered to act as a spy for the French police. He recruited other ex-convicts, who used their knowledge of criminal activity to make a very effective detective force.

THE STRONG ARM OF THE LAW
Tom Smith was a familiar figure in London's West End in the 1850s. He was 6 feet 5 in (1 m 96 cm) tall and weighed over 287 lbs (130 kg). It was said he could stop a fight merely by appearing at the scene.

Stovepipe hat

Tunic collar with officer's identification number

Sheriff badge

Pinkerton detective badge

This staff is tipped with a metal crown

SIGN OF OFFICE
Tipstaffs were used for identification. They were carried by English sheriffs' officers or bailiffs when delivering legal warrants. The officers themselves also became known as "tipstaffs."

Federal marshal badge

BADGES OF OFFICE
Public officials have always needed identification to prove their authority. It is especially important for a law enforcement officer – whether a sheriff in the Wild West or a detective constable in London – to show that he or she has the power to search and arrest.

Embossed jacket buttons

Pinkerton in disguise captures a thief aboard a train

ALLAN PINKERTON
Born in Scotland in 1819, Allan Pinkerton arrived in the United States in the early 1840s. In 1850, he founded Pinkerton's National Detective Agency in Chicago. The agency still exists today. Among other feats, Pinkerton foiled an assassination attempt on Abraham Lincoln.

Frank James's revolver

Tassel from the furnishings at Jesse's funeral

WANTED: JESSE JAMES – DEAD OR ALIVE
Offer of a money reward for the capture of criminals is one method used by law enforcement agencies in an effort to maintain order. Between 1866 and 1892, Jesse James and his brother Frank headed a band of outlaws in the Wild West who robbed banks, trains, and stagecoaches, and killed at least 10 people. A $10,000 reward was offered for Jesse's capture, dead or alive.

Long trousers were worn all year round, whatever the weather

Bullets dug out of a tree near Jesse James's hideout

A piece of Jesse James's coffin. In 1882, Jesse was shot by Bob Ford, a fellow outlaw, for a share in the reward

Justice and sentencing

PILLORY
Putting minor criminals on display for the scorn and amusement of the public was first done by the ancient Greeks and Romans. In medieval times, a pillory was used. It trapped the neck and wrists of the felon. He or she was then displayed in the village square or carried through the town. The public threw rotten vegetables at the criminal; an especially disliked criminal would be pelted with stones.

IN MOST PARTS of the modern world the ideas of *justice* and *sentencing* go hand in hand. *Justice* is simply a means by which punishment can be given fairly according to the crime and the circumstances of the convicted criminal. The *sentence* is the punishment imposed. Most national laws consider crimes of violence against people very serious, and the punishments for these offenses are most severe. In a criminal action, a governmental unit asks the court to try an alleged offender. In the United States, that unit may be the local, state, or federal jurisdiction. For example, murder and robbery are generally state crimes.

The prisoner, in blue, is being held by the arm

CHINESE COURT
A prisoner is being brought before a magistrate in a 16th-century Chinese court. By then, China already had a very efficient legal system based on the laws of Confucius, a famous Chinese philosopher of the first century B.C.

Stroud's chess set and board, drawn inside the cover of his book Avian Anatomy

LYNCHING
Lynching is the illegal killing (usually by hanging) of an accused prisoner by a mob. The lynchers usually think that the suspected offender will escape just punishment. Lynching can include beating, burning, stoning, or hanging.

PASSING THE TIME
During his 54-year stay in prison for murder, Robert Stroud studied the diseases of canaries. He became a leading authority and wrote several books on the subject, including this one. He came to be known as "the Birdman of Alcatraz."

An English barrister, a lawyer who pleads cases in the higher courts

"THE HANGING JUDGE"
The state of Arkansas had become so lawless that in 1875 President Ulysses Grant appointed Isaac Charles Parker as a federal judge in Fort Smith. During his legal career in Jesse James territory, Parker had developed a deep hatred for lawbreakers. In 21 years on the bench, Parker issued more than 160 death sentences, earning him the name "The Hanging Judge."

DEFENSE AND PROSECUTION
In many countries, an accused person is given the chance to have his defense presented to the court by a lawyer. A prosecuting counsel presents the opposite case, maintaining the accused's guilt. A jury, a group of independent, randomly selected people, decides whether or not the prosecution has proven the accused's guilt.

COURTROOM CAPERS
This scene depicts an English police court in the early 19th century. It is possible that the violent young men facing the magistrate were arrested for being drunk and disorderly. Such scenes are extremely rare in today's courts, partly because of the fear of harsher sentences, and partly because of the presence of trained security staff.

Handcuffs used to restrain Ketchum

Prisoner's number

"BLACK JACK" KETCHUM
Ketchum was born in New Mexico in 1866. He formed a gang that specialized in train robberies, but they had little success. "Black Jack" was a heavy drinker, not afraid to use his gun. He was finally arrested after being injured in a shoot-out. He was convicted of the murder of Sheriff Edward Farr and hanged.

GUARD DUTY
Either because of the fierce guards or the ferocious currents surrounding the island, only three inmates ever managed to escape the federal prison at Alcatraz, and they have never been seen or heard of since.

Alcatraz guard's belt buckle

Prisoner's shirt of the type worn in Alcatraz

"THE ROCK"
Alcatraz, the world's most notorious prison, was built on a rocky island in San Francisco Bay. Originally a military prison, "The Rock" served as a federal penitentiary from 1934 to 1963. Dangerous currents around the island made escape impossible. Famous inmates included Al Capone, "Machine Gun" Kelly, and Robert Stroud, "the Birdman of Alcatraz."

Bounty hunters and thief takers

WHETHER BOUNTY HUNTERS in the American Wild West or thief takers in 18th-century Britain, some people have always been ready to catch criminals for a rich reward. There were few sheriffs in the new, 19th-century towns of the United States, so bounty hunters flourished as rough-and-ready peacekeepers. Thief taking became popular in England after the passage of the Highwayman Act in 1692. This act offered large rewards for the capture of highwaymen and other criminals. If the thief takers were criminals themselves, they would be granted a pardon for bringing in the accused. This meant that it was easy for a guilty person to send an innocent one to the gallows.

A pouch of gold and silver coins, the thief taker's "blood money"

THE PAYOFF
Bounty hunters and thief takers were paid well. In Britain, a thief taker earned 40 pounds, and the highwayman's horse and goods, for each convicted thief. In the United States, the bounty hunter's reward depended on the notoriety of the criminal. The first reward offered for the outlaw Jesse James was $500; the last was $25,000.

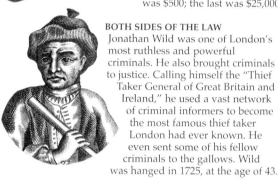

BOTH SIDES OF THE LAW
Jonathan Wild was one of London's most ruthless and powerful criminals. He also brought criminals to justice. Calling himself the "Thief Taker General of Great Britain and Ireland," he used a vast network of criminal informers to become the most famous thief taker London had ever known. He even sent some of his fellow criminals to the gallows. Wild was hanged in 1725, at the age of 43.

An idealized painting of Pat Garrett

BILLY THE KID
Billy the Kid never went to school. Born in New York City in 1859, he was brought up on the legend of Jesse James (p. 11). He became a gambler, a rustler (a cattle and horse thief), and a killer. Billy's real name is believed to be William H. Bonney.

TRACKER
In 1880, Patrick Floyd Garrett, the sheriff of Lincoln County, New Mexico, captured the notorious outlaw Billy the Kid. The Kid escaped from jail but not from Garrett, who tracked him for three months and finally shot him dead at Fort Sumner, New Mexico, in July 1881.

DICK TURPIN
An infamous highwayman, Dick Turpin (1705–1739) robbed coaches on the busy roads near London. He tried to prevent his friend and fellow highwayman Tom King from being captured. In doing so, Turpin accidentally shot King, who later died.

An employee of a bail bondsman

IN CUSTODY
Bounty hunting can still be lucrative. In the United States, if a person is arrested and offered bail, he can borrow the money, called a bail bond, from a bail bondsman for a fee. If the accused does not appear in court, the bondsman loses his money. This is when the bondsman puts bounty hunters on the fugitive's trail to recoup his money.

MODERN BOUNTY HUNTERS
In this photograph, a modern-day bounty hunter catches a criminal in Miami. More than 100 years have passed since the legendary days of the Wild West. Although the preservation of law and order is now firmly in the hands of the FBI and local police forces, independent operators still work for reward money.

Reeder Webb's ivory-handled Colt gun

SHERIFF REEDER WEBB
In 1927, the Texas Bankers' Association published an announcement: "Reward $5,000 for dead bank robbers, not one cent for live ones." According to local legend, Reeder Webb, the sheriff of Odessa, West Texas, then lured two local thieves to a bank, where he shot them and collected the reward. To this day, a picture of Webb hangs in the sheriff's office in Odessa.

Webb's leather-covered blackjack

THE MAN WITH NO NAME
This still is from the 1964 western film *A Fistful of Dollars* in which Clint Eastwood played an honorable bounty hunter. In actuality, bounty hunters in the Wild West were often no more than hired killers, who would murder anyone for a "fistful of dollars."

Sheriff Webb's brass knuckles

Theft and burglary

Suitcases can be used to carry stolen goods from the property

THEFT AND BURGLARY are classified as crimes against property. Theft covers everything from stealing an apple from a fruit stand to lifting a gold watch from a jeweler's counter. A theft is considered to be far more serious if it involves physical violence, as in the case of mugging. Burglary is entering a building for the purpose of stealing. It is considered a very serious crime, especially if the act is aggravated, for example, by the use of a gun.

MAKING A BREAK FOR IT
In 1950, a reformed burglar walked into the office of the English magazine *Picture Post* and offered to demonstrate his skills for an article on the methods used by a burglar. He staged a job and it was photographed. The former burglar stated that the general public, by failing to properly secure their homes, made burglary easy to commit.

COLONEL BLOOD
In England in 1671, Irish adventurer Thomas Blood and two accomplices, disguised as clergymen, were allowed to see the crown jewels in the Tower of London. They attempted to steal them but found most of them too bulky and heavy. Blood managed to escape with the crown, crushed and hidden under his coat. The thieves were captured when Blood's horse fell. King Charles II, impressed by the daring of the plot, gave Blood a royal pardon.

NED KELLY
Born in Australia in 1855, the son of a transported convict, Ned became a bushranger, a robber who lived in the bush, or outback. As the result of a scuffle with a policeman, he and his gang were hunted down by troopers. Only one of the soldiers survived the gun battle. For the next two years, Ned Kelly made a profitable living robbing banks. He is known for a remarkable suit of armor made from iron. He met his death on the gallows in 1880.

Wanted notices

PUBLIC ENEMY NO. 1
In 1933, at the age of 31, John Dillinger had already spent nine years in prison for theft. On his release, he formed a gang and became a notorious bank robber. Soon Dillinger was at the top of the FBI's Public Enemy list, and huge rewards were being offered for his capture, dead or alive. Finally he was betrayed by Anna Sager, an acquaintance, who became known as "the woman in red." The FBI shot Dillinger as he walked out of a movie theater in Chicago in July 1934.

GREAT TRAIN ROBBERY

In the early hours of August 8, 1963, a gang of 12 robbers stole 2.5 million pounds from the Royal Mail train traveling between London, England, and Glasgow, Scotland. They hid out at a remote farmhouse before separating with their shares of the loot. Three of the gang got away. The rest, including the three pictured here, spent lengthy terms in prison.

Train coach

Charlie Wilson

Jimmy White

Bruce Reynolds

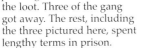

T JOURNAL-STANDARD

FREEPORT, ILLINOIS, MONDAY, JULY 23, 1934   Price Three Cents

LLED BY LAW OFFICERS

ke up Minneapolis Peace Task

FAMOUS OUTLAW COMES TO USUAL END OF HIS KIND

Most Notorious Desperado Slain

TRIO OF VICIOUS KILLERS AT LARGE IN SOUTHWEST

Island Princess To Greet F. D. R.

Headline announcing Dillinger's death

Dillinger's wooden "gun" blackened with shoe polish

DILLINGER'S ESCAPE

In January 1934, Dillinger was arrested in Tucson, Arizona, and sent to Indiana to face charges of killing a poilceman. Always a clever crook, Dillinger escaped from the jail in Crown Point by waving a "gun." In fact his weapon was simply a piece of wood carved into the shape of a gun. It could not have maimed anyone.

WANTED
IN 5 STATES

DIVISION OF INVESTIGATION
U. S. DEPARTMENT OF JUSTICE
WASHINGTON, D. C.

Fingerprint Classification

12 9 R O
14 U 00 9

NATIONAL MOTOR VEHICLE THEFT ACT

Photograph taken January 25, 1930

CRIMINAL RECORD

John Dillinger

The forks can be levered up to here to allow the ram raiders to enter at a higher level

RAM RAIDING

A new threat hit the commercial and business world in the 1990s in the form of ram raiding. Vehicles fitted with fenders made from reinforced steel girders are rammed into doors and windows of shops and warehouses, breaking open an entry for robbers. The industrial vehicle shown above is perfect for the crime because of the forks at the front.

Dillinger's death mask. A mold of his face was made after his death for identification

Drill could not pierce safe

SAFE DEPOSIT BOX OPENER

In 1987, 60 million pounds were stolen from the Kensington Safe Depository Center in London. The robbers took this electric drill to the scene to get into the safes. The drill snapped and was abandoned in favor of sledgehammers. Valerio Viccei, the leader of the robbers, was caught and sentenced to 22 years in prison.

Swindles and frauds

THE WORLD IS A LARGE MARKETPLACE, with people selling goods and services and other people buying them. But this atmosphere of commerce has a dark side to it. Wherever there is a chance to make "easy" money by dishonest means, there are untrustworthy individuals ready to take that chance. And for every criminal, there is a person willing to believe that he or she can get something cheap. A swindle or a fraud involves deliberately cheating someone out of money. They range from cardsharps fixing games at fairs so there is no chance of winning, to con artists who have managed to "sell" public monuments for huge amounts of money.

CHARLIE PEACE
A burglar and murderer of the 19th century, Charlie Peace moved in respectable and wealthy circles. He was able to live this double life because he was a brilliant master of disguise. Even his own family could not recognize him in disguise

THE ULTIMATE BUG KILLER
Many swindlers do their business through newspaper advertisements. One ad published in a U.S. newspaper promised "a method 100% effective against cockroaches." People who sent money received two blocks of wood with the instructions: "Place cockroach on block A. Take block B and strike down hard on block A." Although it worked, the defrauder was still sent to prison.

Block B, which is brought down on the execution block to kill the cockroach

FIXING SPORTS EVENTS
There are many ways to fix sports events, from paying a boxer to take a fall, or a football player to throw a game, to drugging horses to win or lose. Swindlers try to fix sports events because they can make huge amounts of money betting (or by taking bets from others) if they know in advance who is going to win. Most sports are regulated to try to prevent this sort of manipulation from taking place.

AT SEA
False claims on insurance policies have always been a common fraud, usually in the area of merchant shipping. For example, a vessel carrying a shipment of wool would be reported wrecked and the cargo lost. Meanwhile, the ship would dock at another port. The wool would be sold and the ship would be given a new name. The owner of the wool would have the money from its sale and the insurance money for its loss. The ship-owner would still have the ship and the insurance for its loss.

Because of the sophisticate tracking equipment onboar modern cargo shi like this one, it almost impossib to "lose" a vess

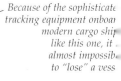

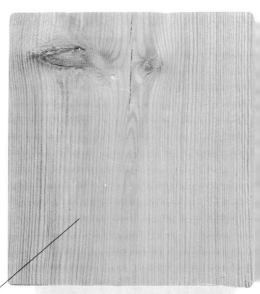

The queen of hearts is turned facedown and shuffled among the other cards

FIND THE LADY
"Find the lady" is a trick played at fairs or on the streets with three cards, one of which is the queen of hearts. The dealer lays the cards facedown on a table, first revealing which one is the queen. He then shuffles the cards on the table and invites the audience to "find the lady." The dealer's accomplice, pretending to be an ordinary onlooker, puts money on a card repeatedly, and wins. Then others try. But without having been briefed by the dealer, they cannot find the queen.

CHARLES PONZI
One of the world's most successful con men, Italian-born Charles Ponzi made a fortune in the United States in 1919–20. He persuaded people to invest money in his Financial Exchange Company with the promise of high interest. In fact, the company was not making any money. The interest it paid out was the money provided by new investors.

Ponzi was convicted of fraud and served nine years in prison

George C. Parker sold the Statue of Liberty

CREDIT CARD FRAUD
The most common form of credit card fraud is the use of stolen cards by thieves, but some schemes are more complex. For example, in the late 1960s, Alphonse Confessore, a maintenance engineer for Diners Club who used to make fraudulent charge cards for his friends, was blackmailed into printing 1,500 fraudulent Diners Club cards for an organized crime gang. Confessore was caught and convicted, then murdered as he left court.

Cockroach on its execution block

VICTORY BONDS
Horatio Bottomley from England was a swindler, publisher, and politician. A self-styled "friend of the poor," he began the Victory Bond Club in Britain in 1919 to let poor people buy a share in the government's postwar investment. In fact, Bottomley was not investing the money, just keeping it for himself. He made £150,000 ($240,000), was accused of fraud, convicted, and sentenced to seven years in prison.

SELLING MONUMENTS
Many of the world's largest and most famous monuments have been "sold" to the gullible by charming tricksters. Probably the greatest "monumental" con man was George C. Parker, who, over 45 years, sold the Brooklyn Bridge, Madison Square Garden, President Grant's tomb, and the Statue of Liberty.

Forgery

THE WORDS *forgery* and *counterfeit* are usually associated with paper money. However, anything that is rare or valuable is likely to be counterfeited, and can include items ranging from ancient Egyptian relics to modern "designer" perfumes. Forgery is usually attempted for profit, prestige, or political reasons. In the time of the Pharaohs, a group of Egyptians created a counterfeit Shabaka Stone, a relic thought to prove that the world was created in their capital city of Memphis. Some counterfeiters, such as those who forge works of art, do so solely to deceive experts. The advance of scientific techniques and instruments have made forgery more detectable than ever before, decreasing a counterfeiter's chance of success.

FORGER AT WORK
Decoration is added to a fake Oriental vase. Chinese porcelain has always been a popular subject for forgers. Even modern artists' ceramic work is often copied.

Gold-covered bronze

GUILTY GOLDEN EAGLE
This pair of fake eagle brooches were made i[n] the 19th century, sometimes known as the gre[at] age of faking. The eagle design was popular i[n] the culture of the Visigoths, a Germanic peop[le] of the second through eighth centuries A.D. Th[e] originals were 4.72 in (12 cm) high and made o[f] solid gold inlaid with precious gems. Sever[al] eagle brooches were analyzed and found to b[e] cast bronze covered with gold sheet and inlai[d] with colored stones. In 1941, Amable Pozo, [a] Spanish jeweler, was revealed as the fake[r].

A fake medieval medallion

Original shabti would have carried hoes; forger mistakenly gave copy flail scepters

CASTING A FORTUNE
Shabti were small figurines that were buried with the dead of ancient Egypt. They were to act as servants and carry out any tasks required of the deceased in the afterlife. Although some fakes have been cast from original shabti, many fakes have been made from scratch. They are easy to detect with their clumsy detail and incorrect hieroglyphic inscriptions.

PLATED FORGERIES
These fake ancient "gold" coins claimed to be from the time of Alexander the Great, were cast in copper and plated in gold. The fraud was exposed only when the plating split to reveal the bright green color of oxidized copper.

Oxidized copper

Fake shabti

Shabti mold

BILLY'S AND CHARLEY'S
In the mid-19th century, Billy Smith and Charley Eaton sold genuine antiquities dug from the Thames foreshore. Demand was so great that they decided to make a few "antiquities" of their own, mostly "medieval" medallions cast in lead. Even after they were revealed as forgers, Billy and Charley continued in business until Charley's death.

THOMAS CHATTERTO[N]
Chatterton, born in 1752, began writing his ow[n] poetry while still at school in England. In 1768, h[e] wrote a fake medieval text that was good enoug[h] to fool local experts. At the age of 18, he travele[d] to London and continued to write fake mediev[al] poems and letters. When some of his work wa[s] revealed as fake, Chatterton lost both fame an[d] fortune. He took his own life with arsenic in 177[0].

COMMERCIAL FORGERY

There was a time when perfume was just perfume. One brand cost about the same as the next to produce. Now certain designer brands have become very desirable and, as a result, cost more than other fragrances. Poor-quality copies of expensive scents are made illegally and are popular.

Out of the bottle, one perfume looks just like another

COPYCAT CURRENCY

Forging currency can be very profitable. The forger can spend the counterfeit money or sell it to other criminals. The many precautions taken today, including paper quality, watermarks, numbering, elaborate engraving and printing processes, and security devices, make it more difficult to produce a forgery that can escape detection. But in earlier times, vast sums of forged currency circulated without detection.

A forged 1835 Bank of Rome note

A genuine 1835 Bank of Rome note

FERNAND LEGROS

Legros is an eccentric French art dealer, recognizable by his signature wide-brimmed hat, beard, and dark glasses. In 1967, he was accused of having sold fake masterpieces to a now-deceased Texas multimillionaire. The canvases were painted by Hungarian forger Elmyr de Hory, who later committed suicide.

A fake Swedish 10-daler note, drawn by hand

Hitler's handwriting

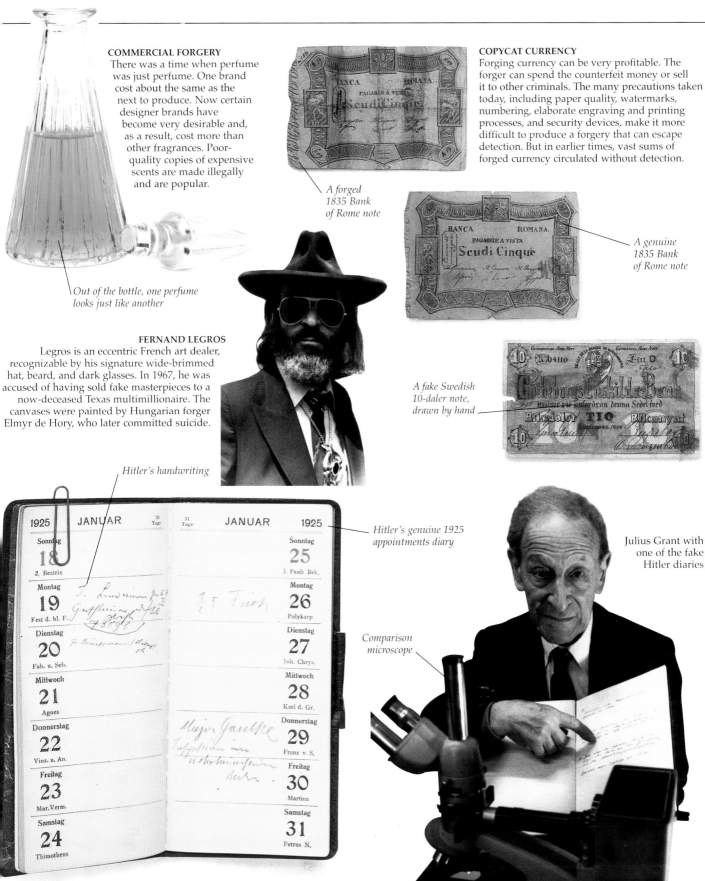

Hitler's genuine 1925 appointments diary

Julius Grant with one of the fake Hitler diaries

Comparison microscope

HITLER'S DIARIES

In 1983, the West German magazine *Stern* announced the discovery of the personal diaries of Adolf Hitler. Many experts lined up to authenticate them. Vast sums of money began to change hands for publication rights. Then Julius Grant, the foremost forensic document examiner of the century, inspected the documents. Grant soon determined that the paper on which the diaries were written contained optical dyes, which were not used in the manufacture of paper until after Hitler's death. Thus the diaries proved to be fakes.

Murder and kidnapping

PEOPLE HAVE BEEN harming and killing each other for property, power, or pleasure since the dawn of time. Other people have been trying to solve these crimes and capture the people responsible for them. As new technology has been developed, so the means of detecting crimes have improved. It is becoming more and more difficult to commit a murder or kidnapping without being caught, especially with advances in forensics (pp. 44–45), but it is often a criminal's own carelessness that leads to his or her apprehension.

"ET TU, BRUTE?"
On March 15, 44 B.C., the Roman emperor Gaius Julius Caesar was stabbed to death in the Senate house by Marcus Brutus and other conspirators because they wanted to seize power. In one of the first triumphs of forensic medicine, Caesar's doctor Antistus was able to state that only one of the 23 stab wounds – the one through the emperor's heart – was fatal.

A page from Le Petit Journal *shows Detective Inspector Walter Dew arresting Crippen and his mistress, who is disguised as a boy*

LINDBERGH ABDUCTION
In March 1932, a notorious baby kidnapping occurred. The baby's father, Charles Lindbergh, was the most famous aviator of his time. A ransom was paid, but on May 12, the infant's dead body was found. He had been killed soon after the abduction.

Serial numbers from bank notes were recorded before Lindbergh handed over the ransom money

One of the investigators Colonel Norman Schwarzkopf (father of General Schwarzkopf of Gulf War fame), recorded details of the Lindbergh case in a diary

CAPTURE OF HAWLEY HARVEY CRIPPEN
After poisoning his wife in 1910, Crippen left London with his mistress, Ethel le Neve, on a ship bound for Canada. Despite the pair's disguises, the captain was suspicious and used the newly invented telegraph system to send a telegram to Scotland Yard. A detective overtook the fugitives on a faster ship and arrested them. Crippen was tried and hanged.

Crippen's pocket watch

HAUPTMANN'S CAPTORS
In September 1934, FBI agents (above) learned that some of Lindbergh's $50,000 ransom money had been used at a New York gas station. The attendant had taken down the license plate number. This led to the arrest of a German-born carpenter named Bruno Hauptmann, who was later tried, found guilty of the child's murder, and executed in 1936.

THE FRENCH "BLUEBEARD"

Henri-Desiré Landru used "lonely hearts" advertisements in French newspapers to meet wealthy women. He then took all their money and property and disappeared. Those women who thwarted his plans were killed. Landru murdered at least 10 women between 1915 and 1919.

Landru and Madame Segret, his mistress at the time he was arrested, who was believed to be his next intended victim

Landru at his trial at the Seine-et-Oise Assize Court in November 1921, before he was convicted and sent to the guillotine in 1922

SADAMICHI HIRASAWA

On January 26, 1948, Sadamichi Hirasawa murdered 12 employees of a Tokyo, Japan, bank. He posed as a Health Department official and told the manager that, because of a dysentery outbreak, all employees must be given a dose of medicine. Within seconds of drinking the cyanide liquid, the bank staff died. Hirasawa fled with 180,000 yen.

Hirasawa, imprisoned for murder

LEOPOLD AND LOEB

In 1924, Nathan Leopold and Richard Loeb, two American teenagers, tried to commit the perfect murder. On May 21, they stabbed 14-year-old Bobby Franks to death and sent his father a ransom note demanding $10,000. Leopold's eyeglasses were dropped near the body. This and other evidence led to the pair's conviction. They were sentenced to life imprisonment for murder and 99 years for kidnapping.

Lord Lucan's House of Lords cloak label

THE EARL OF LUCAN

Lucan's trunk, in which he carried his silver to an auction shortly before he disappeared

THE Rᵗ HONᵇᴸᴱ
THE EARL ᴼᶠ LUCAN
Nº 5.

WHERE IS "LUCKY" LUCAN?

Richard John Bingham, Seventh Earl of Lucan, known as "Lucky" to his friends, disappeared on November 7, 1974. In the home of his former wife, he left the body of Sandra Rivett, his children's nanny. In June 1975, the coroner's jury announced a verdict of "murder by Lord Lucan." Although there have been reports from all over the world that Lord Lucan has been seen alive, the sightings have never been confirmed. His fate remains a mystery!

Prohibition

On October 28, 1919, the U.S. Congress passed the National Prohibition Act, commonly known as the Volstead Act, which made the sale of alcoholic liquor illegal. At first it was a popular act, but soon it was evident that Prohibition was both absurd and unworkable. People who rarely drank became desperate to do so; people who drank a lot demanded more. This demand was being met by organized gangs who had discovered that huge amounts of money could be made. Ships carried cases of spirits to the United States from all over the world. A $15 case of smuggled whisky would be sold for $80. Rivalry between gangs was fierce and often erupted into violence in the streets.

AL "SCARFACE" CAPONE
Alphonse Capone, most notorious of the Chicago gangsters, began his career in crime in New York. In 1919, he took control of illegal alcohol distribution in Chicago. It is claimed that Capone, with 300 gunmen, was responsible for 1,000 killings.

Al Capone's silver cigarette case

Crowd looting a store of confiscated liquor

A sawed-off double-barreled shotgun hidden in a violin case

HIDING THE LIQUOR
Soon the gangs found they could make more cash by manufacturing and selling their own alcohol (bootlegging), and there was less risk involved. However, many people tired of the excessive profits made by the gangsters and decided they too could make their own, known as "bathtub gin." It was not until 1933 that Prohibition was repealed.

THE UNTOUCHABLES
Eliot Ness, born in 1902, became well known during the late 1920s as a special agent in the Prohibition Bureau of the U.S. Department of Justice. He led a team of officers, called "The Untouchables" because they could not be bribed or intimidated by gangsters, to break up the trade in illegal alcohol.

HOOVER
John Edgar Hoover rose through the ranks of the U.S. Department of Justice to become the first director of the Federal Bureau of Investigation (FBI) in 1924. During the 1930s, he attacked the problem of gangsterism and started a list of "Public Enemies." Hoover headed the FBI for 48 years, under eight presidents.

SAM GIANCANA

When Al Capone died, other mobsters, including Sam "Momo" Giancana, took over the Chicago underworld. Giancana later became the city's crime boss. He moved into gambling clubs and ended up with a large share of the Riviera Casino.

Giancana's lucky four-leaf clover

Giancana's lighters

Giancana after his 1957 arrest in Chicago in connection with the murder of banker Leon Marcus

GIANCANA'S JEWELRY

Giancana's jewelry was confiscated and returned by the law when he was arrested many times. Before the age of 20, he had been arrested three times for murder. When he took command of the Chicago Mafia, he had been arrested 60 times for charges including battery, bombing, and assault to kill. He was described as the most ruthless mobster in the United States. He was murdered in his home in 1975.

Giancana's betting book, containing winning slips only, was used as evidence of a legitimate income

CONCEALED THREATS

For obvious reasons, gangsters preferred to conceal their weapons when traveling to a "job." The most popular hiding place for shotguns and the Thompson submachine gun, or tommy gun, was a violin case. It proved surprisingly successful despite the fact that a group of "Big Al's" hoodlums were not likely to pass as the string section of the Chicago Philharmonic!

Details of the various bets Giancana made

Frank Costello, born Francesco Castiglia in Lauropolin, Italy, became known as the "prime minister" of the mob

FRANK COSTELLO

Frank Costello rose through the gangster world to control much of the country's gambling. In 1951, he was a star witness at the Kefauver Investigation. Despite the extent of his gangland crime, Costello, like Capone, was finally jailed for tax evasion.

KEFAUVER HEARINGS

The televised hearings were opened in May 1950 by Tennessee's Senator Estes Kefauver. The five-man committee spent almost two years traveling the United States interviewing hundreds of underworld figures to determine whether there was any evidence that an organized crime syndicate was in operation. Their conclusion was that such a network did exist.

International gangsters

THE MAFIA IS PROBABLY THE BEST-KNOWN organized crime gang in the world, but it is not the only one. Wherever dishonest money can be made from drugs, gambling, and moneylending, gangsters organize themselves into powerful groups to lay claim to it. Like the mobsters of Prohibition times, modern gangsters defend their territory jealously, and often violently, and new territories are constantly established. For example, the Triads, which originated in China, now have units all around the world. However, there have been great changes in the way that these modern criminals operate. Gangsters often look more like bank managers than hoodlums, and many have come to realize that there is a considerable advantage in running a respectable business to act as a cover for their dishonest deals.

MAFIA NUN
Sister Alvina Murelli, a 51-year-old nun, was arrested in 1983, in Naples, Italy, when police began a crackdown on the underworld of organized crime gangs. In the photo above, she holds a copy of the New Testament's four Gospels. She used this book to smuggle out coded messages from the mafiosi whom she visited in jail.

MONEY LAUNDERING
The main source of wealth for most gangs is the illegal trade in drugs. Drug barons usually launder their "dirty" money by filtering the cash through large "respectable" companies and banks owned or run by the gangs.

Paddle for turning cards

GAMBLING
Like the drug trade, illegal gambling is a popular source of gangland money. It provides very big returns for very little outlay, and the chances of winning are stacked against the player even if the game has not been fixed. Chinese games of chance figure very strongly in the Triad economy, and illegal basement gambling dens can be found in Chinatown districts around the world.

Card dispenser ensures that dealer's hands barely touch cards

Betting counters, called chips

Gambling cards

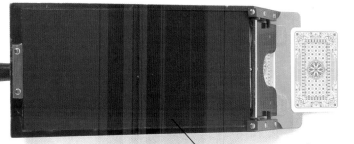

YAKUZA FUNERAL
The Yakuza controls most of the gangland activity in Japan. Although the members claim to have a Robin Hood image – robbing the rich to give to the poor – the Yakuza was officially outlawed in 1992 for its activities in the areas of extortion, money laundering, and gunrunning. In 1984, Masahisa Takenaka, leader of the Yamaguchi-gumi (largest of the Yakuza gangs), was killed by rivals. His funeral (left) was attended by members of the group – and 400 riot police.

Masahisa Takenaka

Giovanni Brusca was
arrested at a seaside
resort in Sicily

Doorway and
steps carved
out of stone

CAPTURING GANGSTERS

Enhanced communications systems around
the globe have increased the efficiency and
success rate of most of the world's police
forces. In 1996, the arrest of Sicilian bomber
Giovanni Brusca ended one of Italy's
most intensive manhunts and marked
a significant victory against the growing
threat of organized crime in Sicily and Italy.

Roulette wheels
are often rigged
so the operator
can control where
the ball drops

SECRET HIDEAWAYS

Communication among Mafia bosses
has also improved over the years,
and many meetings are held to
arrange "business" deals. In 1985,
Italian police broke into caves under
the country villa of Michele Greco,
a top Mafia leader in Sicily. Mafia
leaders held summit meetings in
this underground hideaway.

"RUSSIAN MAFIA"

In the confusion and disarray
following the breakup of the
former Soviet Union, organized
crime moved in. Known as the
"Russian mafia," the gangs have
become ruthless, violent and
increasingly bold. This violence
has been met with equal brutality
by the police – resulting in many
funerals, such as that of mobster
Vladislav Listiev (above).

ALL ON THE SPIN OF A WHEEL

One of the most popular gambling
games in the big casinos is roulette.
For decades, organized crime has made
easy money at the roulette wheel, where
corrupt casino owners run rigged games.
Most of the profitable betting games,
however, are card games, such
as blackjack, poker, and faro.

Gamblers
bet on where
the ball will stop

Gambling chip

Chip sweep
to gather
in chips

Smuggling and piracy

SMUGGLING IS THE ILLEGAL MOVEMENT of goods in and out of countries. It is an extremely profitable crime because the smuggler avoids paying customs duties on these items. Customs duties are taxes on certain goods, such as tobacco or alcohol, that are imported into the country. There is also a profit to be made when smuggling items or substances that are banned, such as illegal drugs like cocaine and marijuana, from one country to another. Piracy, or robbery at sea, has occurred since ancient times, and involves the capture of wealth or vessels on the open seas.

OLDEST TRICK IN THE BOO
An old method of smuggling small amounts illegal goods is to hide them inside a hollowed out section of a book. Another method replacing a legal substance, such as talcu powder, with a similar-looking illegal dru

Mandolin made from illegally exported turtle shell

CUSTOMS OFFICERS
Port police officers, such as these French officers in 1905 (above), are called customs officers and work to prevent smuggling. Alcohol and tobacco used to be commonly smuggled substances. Now drugs are a customs officer's main concerns.

FACE THE WALL
It was customary for villagers of the south coast of England during the 18th century to turn their faces to the wall when smugglers carried contraband from their boats. This way, the locals could not identify the smugglers when questioned by customs officers. Identification would both anger the smugglers and deprive the locals of the smuggled goods.

ON THE EDGE OF EXTINCTION
As a result of the continuing threat to endangered wildlife, international agreements have been signed to outlaw the killing of certain birds and animals. Also banned are the export of some live creature and the trade in animal parts, such as skins, ivory, and bones. The exquisite shell of the hawksbill turtle (left) is sold illegally as a curiosity or for making into souvenirs such as jewelry boxes.

Shell of hawksbill turtle

SKIN OF THE JAGUAR
The jaguar is killed illegally for its coat. This skin was seized by authorities in Brazil. In many parts of the world, trade in illegal animal products provides an income that is vital for human survival. Where conservation is most needed, poverty is often greatest.

BAG CHECKING
While armed officers secure the safety of a seaport or airport, customs officers inspect passengers' baggage for smuggled goods. They usually do not check every suitcase or bag, but rely on experience, instinct, or tips (advance information) to pick out bags likely to contain smuggled goods.

X-RAY VISION
In an attempt to reduce international terrorism and smuggling, officers use equipment that can scan human beings and their luggage for concealed objects, such as guns. This device has detected bags of cocaine, knives (plastic and metal), coins, and guns.

Space in a pair of boots to hide drugs

WAYS ON ALERT
...uggling is only one of the ...mes that air transport police ...ust try to prevent. Others ...clude terrorism and large-scale ...eft from the airport's secure ...arehouses. Airports are policed ...y armed security officers.

HIDING THE GOODS
Getting contraband (smuggled goods) past the watchful eyes of customs officers is the smuggler's most difficult task. Countless objects have been used to conceal forbidden contraband – from hollowed-out books and statues to shoes and spare tires.

...hollowed-out ...ulpture

Hollow heel in a shoe

Drum ready to be filled with drugs

PIRATES
A gang of Chinese pirates (above) climb aboard to attack a ship. Pirates were not the romantic characters portrayed in literature and films. They were murderous robbers who often fought among themselves and stole from each other.

Fire!

Most fires start accidentally – a cigarette is left burning, or a stove is left on. Arson fires, however, are started deliberately. Whatever the cause of the fire, the procedure to put it out is the same. Most countries have emergency fire departments. When the firefighters arrive at the scene, they must make sure that any occupants are taken to safety, put out the fire, and ensure that the building is safe from collapse. If there has been any loss of life, or if the fire seems to have been started deliberately, a fire investigation unit moves in. If arson is suspected because, for example, traces of gasoline have been found, the fire investigation unit works closely with the regular police force to solve the crime.

FIGHTING THE FIRE
Firefighters belong to one of the most dangerous of the emergency services. At each major incident there are three major hazards – fire and explosion, smoke inhalation, and falling debris. The firefighters' skill is enhanced by the use of well-equipped vehicles and advanced protective clothing.

Glass storage jars are used for fire debris samples because glass, unlike plastic, does not contain chemicals that could contaminate samples

SAMPLE COLLECTIO
Collecting clues is vital to t success of any investigatio Because contaminate samples are useless f analysis in the forens laboratory (pp. 46–47), office carry glass jars in which store and protect evidenc

Knob to adjust hydrogen gas flow

Reading shows how flammable the gas is

TESTING THE AIR FOR GASES
Once the fire is out, the fire investigation unit tries to find the cause. The hydrogen flame tester is used to detect the presence of flammable gases at the scene of a fire. Once it is established that a flammable gas is present, the gas can be identified and the cause of the fire determined. Within the machine, there is a naked hydrogen flame. Gas is sucked in and passes over this flame. The flame increases if the gas is flammable, and this increase is translated into a meter reading. The degree of flammability indicates the nature of the gas.

Hydrogen gas supply

Gas is sucked into the machine through this nozzle

Gas enters small holes along this tube

Fire investigators connect this attachment to the nozzle when they are detecting gases in awkward places, such as along ceilings or floors

REASONS FOR ARSON

There are three main reasons for arson. The fire may disguise some other crime, such as robbery or murder. It may be started as an act of revenge. However, most arson attacks are associated with fraud. The number of arson fires rose during the Great Depression in the United States in the 1930s as financially troubled businesses burned their property to collect insurance payments.

Some people, like this man selling apples, did not resort to arson to raise money during the Depression

Sonic measurer

HEDGEHOG DISASTER

In Germany in 1954, Dr. Müller and his wife were driving home. Müller claimed that while he left the car to remove a hedgehog from the road, the vehicle burst into flames, killing his wife. Remains of a gasoline can found in the car and proof that Müller had been having a love affair suggested arson. Müller was found guilty of murder and sentenced to six years in prison.

IDENTIFYING THE GASES

Officers use Dräger tubes to identify gases in the air. A tube of chemicals is inserted in the pump. Air is sucked through the tube by pressing the pump. If a gas is present, the chemicals will change color. The gas is identified by comparison to a color chart.

Color change suggests gasoline fumes in the air

Pre-test tube shows the presence of a hydrocarbon – it does not identify it

Tube to identify hydrocarbons, such as paraffin or gasoline fumes

Indicates concealed, potentially dangerous, electrical wires, to be avoided when searching for clues

Metal detector

KING MEASUREMENTS

e accurate recording of a crime scene is sential to all investigations. This is especially portant in the case of arson, where buildings ay have to be quickly demolished for safety asons. Measurements indicate the size and mension of a location and the distance between jects. By comparing these measurements to the tent of fire damage, the officers can determine e speed and nature of the fires. A number of ecialized measuring tools have been developed give very accurate results. The sonic measurer nds sonic rays from one surface to another, easuring the distance in between.

External calipers

Vernier calipers

Magnifying glass with light

FINDING THE SOURCE OF THE FIRE

If the fire investigation unit suspects that the fire was started deliberately, a scene-of-crime officer who specializes in cases of arson is brought in. Since fires spread upward, the officer will begin at the lowest point to find the source of the fire. These officers are looking for clues near a window where an arsonist may have entered or left the building.

eter reading dicates the quantity flammable gas

Long rubber tube (through which the air passes) can reach into inaccessible places

PORTABLE GAS ALARM

The portable gas alarm detects gases in the air before they are present in large enough quantities to be a fire risk. It is used in work environments that are prone to leaking toxic gases, and also by fire investigation units to ensure that the atmosphere in which they are working is safe. The hydrogen flame tester (left) is not used until it has been established that there is not enough gas in the air to cause an explosion when the naked flame is lit.

In addition to operating positions, the device has Battery and Alarms settings, which enable the user to check that it is working properly

Squeezing this bulb sends the air through the alarm system

Police uniforms

THERE ARE TWO IMPORTANT reasons why police officers wear uniforms: first, so they can be recognized by members of the public who need assistance, and by suspects being pursued; and second, so they can identify each other and be identified by other emergency service personnel, such as firefighters, at the scene of an incident. Because climates differ throughout the world, police in different forces have different uniforms. However, all uniforms are designed to be comfortable and functional while still being formal.

Gendarme

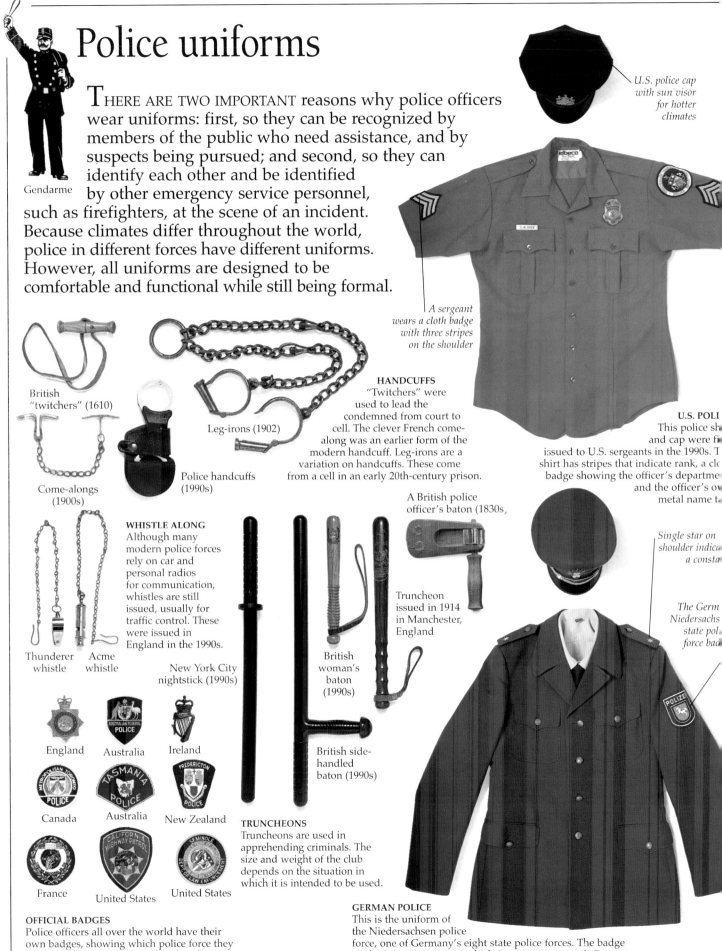

U.S. police cap with sun visor for hotter climates

A sergeant wears a cloth badge with three stripes on the shoulder

British "twitchers" (1610)

Come-alongs (1900s)

Leg-irons (1902)

Police handcuffs (1990s)

HANDCUFFS
"Twitchers" were used to lead the condemned from court to cell. The clever French come-along was an earlier form of the modern handcuff. Leg-irons are a variation on handcuffs. These come from a cell in an early 20th-century prison.

U.S. POLI
This police sh and cap were fi issued to U.S. sergeants in the 1990s. T shirt has stripes that indicate rank, a clo badge showing the officer's departme and the officer's ow metal name ta

Single star on shoulder indica a consta

A British police officer's baton (1830s,

Truncheon issued in 1914 in Manchester, England

The Germ Niedersachs state pol force bac

WHISTLE ALONG
Although many modern police forces rely on car and personal radios for communication, whistles are still issued, usually for traffic control. These were issued in England in the 1990s.

Thunderer whistle

Acme whistle

New York City nightstick (1990s)

British woman's baton (1990s)

British side-handled baton (1990s)

England

Australia

Ireland

Canada

Australia

New Zealand

France

United States

United States

TRUNCHEONS
Truncheons are used in apprehending criminals. The size and weight of the club depends on the situation in which it is intended to be used.

OFFICIAL BADGES
Police officers all over the world have their own badges, showing which police force they represent. These cloth badges are attached to the officers' modern-day uniforms.

GERMAN POLICE
This is the uniform of the Niedersachsen police force, one of Germany's eight state police forces. The badge on the left arm indicates which force is represented. One star on the shoulder indicates that the officer is a constable.

Wide-brimmed Mountie's hat

WOMEN ON THE BEAT
This uniform is worn by a British woman police constable (WPC). The first female officers appeared on the streets in 1919, following the success of their voluntary patrols during World War I. They are now familiar sights as they patrol the streets in company with a male officer. A female officer must generally be in attendance when a female suspect is arrested, questioned, or searched.

Hard hat, suitable for riot conditions

...nyard, or ...rd, that ...lds gun

...m Browne ...ather belt) ...d pouch

Handbag holds WPC's truncheon

Traditional scarlet tunic used for ceremonial occasions – working uniform is brown

Gun holster

...OUNTIES
...his familiar red ...nic of the Royal Canadian Mounted Police was ...sed in 1972. In 1873, when the mounted police force ...as created, Mounties not only upheld the law but ...so acted as local counselors ...d mediators. Their ...nage has slowly ...anged and ...eveloped and, in ...974, women joined ...e Mounties.

Modern jackets and shirts are more tailored than earlier, bulky uniforms

Headwear of a woman officer of the rank of assistant chief constable

Cap of the Russian militia

...lver badge ...' the militia

British woman's police hat

Indian police cap

British police helmet

British (1830s)   French (1920s)   Italian (1990s)

FROM OLD TO NEW
Although the job of the police – to keep the peace – has remained the same through time, both the uniforms and technology available for use in the fight against crime have advanced a great deal. Compare the truncheon of the 1830s with the gun of the 1990s.

...USSIAN
...his cap and ...nic belonged to a major in the Russian militia in 1989. The ...ilitia was responsible for policing Russia both before and ...ter the breakup of the former Soviet Union in 1991. After ...91, Russia had to combat a huge rise in organized crime.

Police agencies

Sheriff's badge

Hungarian warrant card

IDENTIFICATION
All officers must carry identification. It is especially important for plain-clothes officers. The identification displays the officer's credentials and photograph.

MOST PEOPLE THINK of police as either uniformed patrol officers who keep the peace on the world's streets or detectives who solve serious crimes. In fact, police forces include many specialized units formed to operate in special circumstances and conditions. Some squads, such as the Japanese riot police, the French Compagnies Republicaines de Sécurité (CRS), and the U.S. Special Weapons and Tactics (SWAT) units, are trained to deal with difficult violent situations. Some squads use specialized vehicles, such as helicopters, boats, motorcycles, or horses, to perform their job under unusual conditions. The overall aim is to develop a chain of interdependent units to combat crime.

ON THE BEA
A community's safety and well-beir are usually in the hands of the "bea officers such as the French policema here. A beat police officer patro the streets on foot or in a vehicl preventing crime ar protecting citizens' righ to a crime-free societ

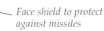

Face shield to protect against missiles

RECOVERING EVIDENCE
Many criminals seem to believe they can destroy evidence – such as a weapon – by throwing it into a canal or river. However, most police forces have trained diving units comprised of officers called frogmen. Ninety-five percent of a frogman's work is done in zero visibility, relying entirely on touch. Divers recover not only weapons but also vehicles and bodies.

Underwat breathir apparat

Armor to protect hands in close combat

Possible murder weapon

CROWD CONTROL
In any situation where rioting crowds cannot be managed by regular police, specially trained and equipped officers are sent to the scene to restore order. In Japan, the riot police squad (above) is known for its efficiency.

HIGHWAY PATROL
High speed and maneuverability have made motorcycles an essential vehicle for the police. Most forces have trained motorcycle units, such as the Los Angeles traffic police (left), who patrol the highways and city streets.

POLICE MARKSMEN

Officers highly trained in the use of firearms work with the regular police in sieges or hostage situations. The order to shoot to kill is only given when all other options have failed, as there is always a chance of hitting a civilian. These special armed units are separate from the many officers throughout the world who routinely carry guns.

High-velocity rifle with telescopic sight

Safety helmet

MOUNTAIN RESCUE

Special police teams with climbing experience are used in some mountain areas to help with rescue work. The officers (above) work in the French Alps where they use motorcycles to travel quickly over rough ground. The motorcycles are much lighter than those used in highway patrol, similar to the trail bikes used in cross-country racing.

Officer's raincoat is kept in this leather pouch

...olice horses are exposed to ...ud recordings of crowds ...nd bands to get ...em used to noise

Riders spend half their working week grooming horses and cleaning their equipment

...OUNTED POLICE

...lany countries have a ...ounted police branch, ...sually used to control ...rowds and to perform ...eremonial duties. The first ...ritish horse patrol was a ...air of mounted Bow Street ...unners (p. 10) in 1763. In 1805, a ...rger patrol was introduced. Because ... the color of their jackets, the officers ...vere called "Robin Redbreasts." Today ...ondon's Metropolitan Police has a ...atrol of about 200 horses. A female ...der is shown here (right).

Long baton used in riot control

...ANADIAN MOUNTIES

...he Royal Canadian Mounted Police was founded ... 1873 as the North West Mounted Police, then ...named in 1920. The Mounties patrolled the vast ...rairies in the west. The intelligence and sure-...ootedness of the horse made it a perfect means of ...ansport. Even today, the horse is a valuable asset.

Selected horses are three- to four-year-old hunters. Like their riders, they receive about two years' training

Detectives

THE TASKS OF INVESTIGATING a crime and identifying the culprit are carried out by detectives. Whether by interviewing witnesses or searching for the tiniest piece of forensic evidence, detectives try to reconstruct a sequence of events until they believe they know what happened. Most detectives are officers in a specialized division of the police, but many others work for private agencies. These detectives, who are often known as private investigators (PI's), can be hired by anybody to investigate anything – for a fee. The public's fascination with the detection of crime is reflected in the number of detective stories in books and on film and television. These detectives may be real or fictional characters, and their methods and equipment may differ, but they share a common pursuit: the fight against crime.

SIR ARTHUR CONAN DOYLE
Probably the world's best-known fictional detective is Sherlock Holmes, created in the 1880s by Sir Arthur Conan Doyle (1859–1930), a British writer. Holmes relied on logical deduction and attention to minute detail to solve crimes. It is less well known that Conan Doyle was also an amateur sleuth himself, and was involved in a number of major cases.

TAKING A CLOSE LOOK
Sometimes the smallest detail provides the clue that solves a crime, which is why the ability to magnify objects is so important in detection. In the laboratory, microscopes are among the most valuable pieces of equipment. Binoculars are also useful to detectives on surveillance, who must be able to see activities and people clearly without being noticed themselves.

Binoculars used by a private investigator

This knob adapts the degree of magnification to suit the user's vision

A scene-of-crime officer with a magnifying lens can identify small clues, such as hairs or cloth fibers

MAIGRET
Popular French detective Commissaire Jules Maigret of the Police Judiciaire is the main character of dozens of novels, short stories, films, and television programs.
Maigret was created in 1930 by Georges Simenon, a Belgian-born writer, and has always been identifiable by his trademark pipe.

INTERNATIONAL AGENCY
Police forces around the world are centralized at Interpol (the International Criminal Police Organization), established in 1923. Police detectives can refer to computer files, fingerprints, and criminal records gathered from more than 100 member countries. Interpol headquarters have been in Lyon, France, since 1989.

PHILIP MARLOWE
A familiar character in detective fiction is the hard-boiled, tough-talking private eye who lives a lonely life on the city's "mean streets." Philip Marlowe, created in the 1930s by Raymond Chandler, is perhaps the best-known example of the type, immortalized in novels and films.

MRS. KERNER
Annette Kerner, Britain's most famous female private detective, worked from the early 1920s to the 1950s. She became known as "the queen of disguise" and was equally convincing as a waitress in a criminals' café as she was as a socialite while thwarting a jewel theft. She once posed as a drug addict to catch a gang of opium dealers.

Allan Pinkerton

PRIVATE EYES THAT NEVER SLEEP
In 1850, U.S. detective Allan Pinkerton established the organization that has become the world's oldest privately owned detective agency – it is still going strong. The term *private eye* came from the Pinkerton trademark – the words "We Never Sleep" written under an open eye.

USING CRIME AGAINST CRIMINALS
It is not only burglars who find it useful to have a set of tools to open locks. Many detectives and undercover surveillance officers also need to get past locked doors – perhaps in the search for drugs, stolen goods, or information about a crime. The official equipment shown at left can open most kinds of locks, almost anywhere in the world.

Selection of lock-picks

File

Keyway blank

Special telephoto lens for long-distance work

Tool for probing locks

Camera's standard lens

RECORDING EVIDENCE
All investigations involve the collection of a wide range of clues. Photographs are vital. They may record a meeting between the individuals under investigation, a crime in progress, or the scene of a crime that has not yet been disturbed by investigators. Most private detectives will use a telephoto lens, like the one at right, to gather evidence from a distance.

PSYCHIC DETECTION
Estelle Roberts was a famous English "psychic detective" who worked with the police. If given a victim's personal objects from the crime, Roberts could sometimes imagine the crime scene in her head, even seeing the criminal's face.

Undercover surveillance

INFORMATION IS VITAL to both the person who wants to commit a crime and the person who wants to catch the criminal. For example, the time at which a bank transfers money is as important to the bank robber as the time of a planned raid is to the law enforcement officer. In the early days of detective work, information-gathering techniques were simple. The robber, sometimes working with an accomplice inside the bank, watched and waited. The officer, with the help of informants, did the same. Today's great technological advances, however, have made the gathering of secret information easier than ever. With round-the-clock observation on closed-circuit television, telephone tapping using tiny transmitters, and advanced tracking systems that lead detectives to the thief, criminals may be seen, heard, and traced through every stage of their crimes.

THE EVER-OPEN EYE
The use of closed-circuit television (CCTV) is vit. in the fight against crim. Signals are transmitted from a camera to a television screen along cables or telephone links, in a closed circuit. Cameras placed in areas such as stores and banks can provide police with accurate records of crimes being committed and lead to visual identification of the perpetrators. The introduction of CCTV in courtrooms allows some witnesses, such as young children, to be interviewe in a separate room with a live video replay in the courtroo

WIRED FOR SOUND
This battery-operated bug (below left) is the size of a matchbox. The device, which consists of a microphone attached to a radio transmitter, is hidden. Sound signals from the bug are picked up by the radio receiver (below right), which transfers the signals to an earpiece.

A BUGGED ELECTRIC SOCKET
This electric socket looks like any other. Even with the cover removed, the miniature bugging device is not visible. The device is a transmitter that carries sound in the room, in the form of radio waves, to a distant receiving unit. Another kind of device transmits sound directly along the power cable to a receiver plugged into the same electrical circuit.

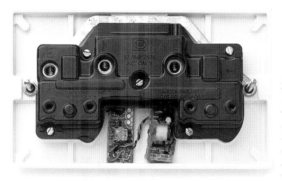

Radio receiver with earpiece

CONCEALED CAMERA
This canvas shoulder bag has been adapted to hide a video camera. One of the fasteners has been removed, leaving a hole. The camera is carefully placed inside the bag so that the lens is positioned next to the hole. The concealed camera can then secretly record images from within the bag.

Ordinary canv. sports b.

The bag filled wi clothing protect t. camera ar hold it positic

Main body of b. has a hole in through whi. the camera le. receives an ima.

Normal-size lens. Some cameras have lenses as small as match heads

Wallet with transmitter

Magnet to cancel alarm

This wire clips to a document and activates an alarm if the document is disturbed

Alarm

Radio receiver

HIGH-TECH PURSE
If this wallet is moved, a radio transmitter triggers an alarm system. A thief trying to lift the purse from a bag or drawer would be detected immediately. A magnet passed across the wallet cancels the alarm.

Magnetic strip

DESK TRAP
These devices alert people to thieves attempting to steal from desk drawers. The lower device has two magnets joined by a wire. One magnet is stuck to the underside of the desk, the other to the top of the drawer. If the drawer is opened, the magnetic field is broken, setting off an alarm.

UV paste, which sticks well to metal

Cotton swabs for applying powders

Paintbrush for applying pastes

UV crayons for marking furniture or boxes

Gloves to protect detective's hands when applying substances

UV powder for wood or paper objects

Blue UV powder, used on blue objects

UV pen

Powders are visible when concentrated, but invisible once applied

Tweezers for holding bills or coins during application

STAKEOUT
A stakeout is an undercover surveillance operation. In this still from the film *Stakeout*, actor Richard Dreyfuss portrays a detective keeping watch. He uses binoculars, wiretaps, and other classic devices to keep crucial witnesses and suspects under surveillance.

ULTRAVIOLET DETECTOR KIT
One way to fool burglars is to mark valuable goods with a substance that is invisible under normal lighting but that shows up clearly under ultraviolet light. The thief's hands are covered with the substance after handling the goods. Another method is to use a substance that is colorless until it mixes with water. The thief touches the goods and unwittingly covers his or her hands with the substance. Gradually moisture from the hands causes a reaction and the substance becomes visible as a colored stain. Ultraviolet markers are used to write the owner's name on their possessions. If the goods are stolen and then recovered, the owner can be contacted.

Telephone tap

Tap connected to chosen line

Radio transmitter

TAPPING INTO CONVERSATIONS
It is often useful for law enforcement officials to gain access to an individual's telephone conversations. One method of tapping is to connect wires and a transmitter to the junction box outside the building. Another method is to fit a radio transmitter directly into the telephone handset, sending conversations to a receiver set.

Crime scene

THE LOCATION OF A criminal incident is called the scene of the crime. The first job of police officers at the crime scene is to seal off the area so that potential evidence is not disturbed. Once this has been done, only authorized persons are allowed within the area. The most important members of the investigation team at this point are the scene-of-crime officers (SOCOs), who use their extensive training and experience to search for clues to be sent to the forensic laboratory for examination (pp. 46–47). Forensic science is the technique of using scientific methods to solve crimes. Modern forensic science had its origin in 1910, when Edmond Locard of France formulated his "exchange principle." This theory simply states that a criminal always takes something away from the scene of the crime – or leaves something behind. The criminal may take away hair or blood from the victim, or soil (peculiar to the area) on the soles of his or her shoes. The criminal may leave fingerprints, footprints, or fibers from clothing. It is this evidence that the SOCOs collect.

MURDER!
In the case of murder, the body of the victim must be removed from the crime scene and taken for a postmortem as soon as possible. Before this can happen, the victim must be pronounced dead by a doctor. Then a forensic pathologist makes a preliminary examination. Next, a chalk or tape outline is made around the corpse so that investigators know its position. The body can then be transported to the hospital mortuary, where the autopsy takes place.

Toothed calipers enable a tight grip on wet or slippery articles

HUNTING FOR CLUES
This picture shows the hunt for information at the scene of a murder in New York. Nothing in the room has been touched or moved to allow scene-of-crime experts and photographers to record as many details of the crime as possible. A police photographer is recording relevant evidence on film, while his colleague searches for evidence that may be sent to the forensic laboratory.

THE AMPEL PROBE
This tool was designed for use by crime scene investigators. The tongs enable officers to search suspects or their property without risking personal injury (for example, from an open knife) and without damaging objects that may bear trace evidence such as fingerprints. It also is useful for removing evidence without personal contact.

Specially designed handles ensure firm grip

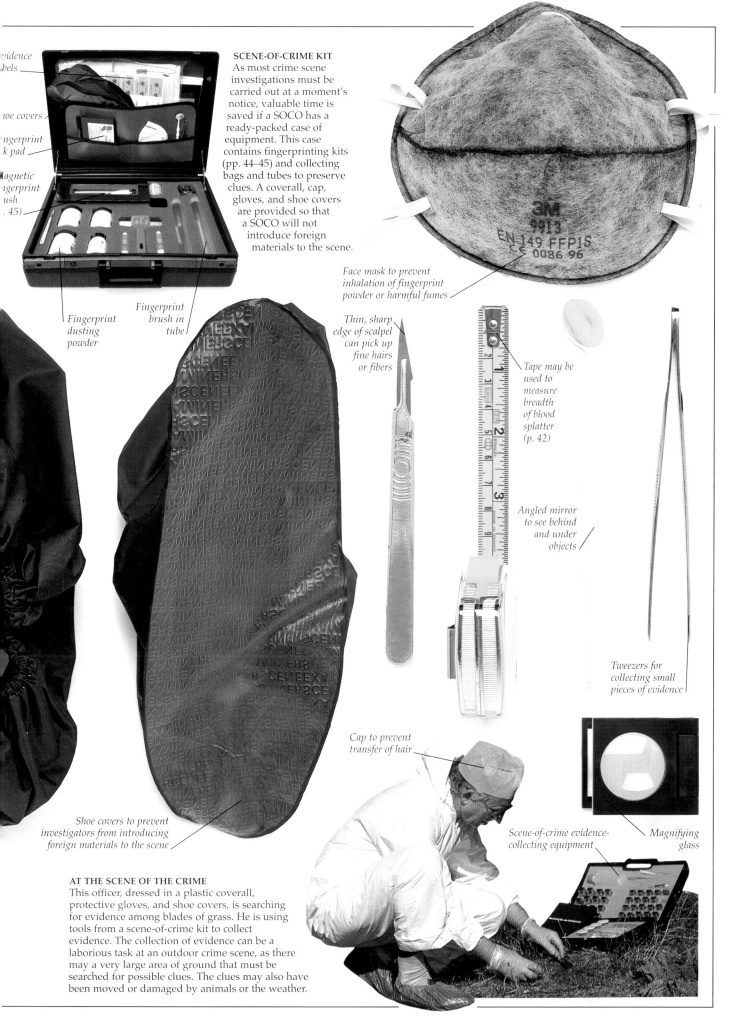

evidence
labels

shoe covers

Fingerprint
ink pad

Magnetic
fingerprint
brush
(p. 45)

SCENE-OF-CRIME KIT
As most crime scene
investigations must be
carried out at a moment's
notice, valuable time is
saved if a SOCO has a
ready-packed case of
equipment. This case
contains fingerprinting kits
(pp. 44–45) and collecting
bags and tubes to preserve
clues. A coverall, cap,
gloves, and shoe covers
are provided so that
a SOCO will not
introduce foreign
materials to the scene.

Fingerprint
dusting
powder

Fingerprint
brush in
tube

Face mask to prevent
inhalation of fingerprint
powder or harmful fumes

Thin, sharp
edge of scalpel
can pick up
fine hairs
or fibers

Tape may be
used to
measure
breadth
of blood
splatter
(p. 42)

Angled mirror
to see behind
and under
objects

Tweezers for
collecting small
pieces of evidence

Cap to prevent
transfer of hair

Scene-of-crime evidence-
collecting equipment

Magnifying
glass

Shoe covers to prevent
investigators from introducing
foreign materials to the scene

AT THE SCENE OF THE CRIME
This officer, dressed in a plastic coverall,
protective gloves, and shoe covers, is searching
for evidence among blades of grass. He is using
tools from a scene-of-crime kit to collect
evidence. The collection of evidence can be a
laborious task at an outdoor crime scene, as there
may a very large area of ground that must be
searched for possible clues. The clues may also have
been moved or damaged by animals or the weather.

Following clues

SEEMINGLY INSIGNIFICANT traces left at the scene of a crime by the victim or criminal are vital clues that can help police in their investigations. Fingerprints, tire prints, and shoe prints can help identify a criminal; bloodstains can illustrate where or how the crime took place. Investigating officers carefully analyze every aspect of a crime scene, even clues that might not be noticed by an untrained person. More dramatic clues, such as bullet holes and broken glass, are easily noticed, but special training and equipment are needed to analyze this kind of evidence. The damage caused by weapons can also provide clues. For example, a piece of glass shattered by a bullet may leave traces on a criminal's clothes.

DROPS OF BLOOD
Marks left by blood can reveal much to the specially trained crime scene investigator. The shape of blood drops on a flat surface can indicate from what height they fell. Splashes on a wall can show the direction from which they came. Other patterns are spurts, pools, smears, and trails. These may reveal the movements of the victim and criminal, and help investigators piece together the crime.

The fired bullet is propelled along the barrel, picking up marks on its way

Marks left on the cartridge, caused by the firing pin when the gun is fired

BULLET MARKS
Cartridges consist of two parts: bullets and cases. When a gun is fired, the bullet travels along the barrel and picks up marks unique to that gun, which can be compared with a test bullet fired from the same weapon. Marks left on the base of the case by the firing pin can be compared in the same way. By comparing bullet marks, investigators can connect a particular weapon to a particular crime.

SHOE PRINTS
Shoe prints are left either as impressions in a substance such as soil, or as prints in a liquid such as blood or oil. These traces are photographed at the scene for future comparison with the shoes of a suspect. Identification points may be the patterns on the sole and distinctive signs of wear and tear.

TIRE PRINTS
Prints left by tires can be compared with the tires on a suspect's car. Like shoes, tires often have an identifiable wear pattern. Police are further helped by the fact that manufacturers use different types of tires on different models of car.

SHOTS THROUGH GLA
Ballistics is the study of guns and ammunitic In a forensic laboratory specializing in ballisti experts set up tests to demonstrate the effe caused by bullets fired from differe distances and through differe thicknesses of glass (above). Poli can refer to this information wh they examine a bullet hole glass from a crime scene can indicate the spot fro which the gun was fir

Broken pattern in tire print suggests that two treads on the outer edge of the tire have worn down

BREAKING GLASS

When glass is smashed, the broken edges have tiny shell-shaped notches. A broken window can be fitted together like a jigsaw puzzle. A piece of glass discovered in a suspect's car can be compared to glass recovered from the crime scene. If the notches fit exactly, the glass is from the same windowpane.

REFRACTIVE INDEX

Tiny pieces of glass found on a suspect's clothing may be too small to fit into a glass jigsaw. Instead, the recovered glass can be compared to glass from the crime scene by measuring its refractive index, or the amount a ray of light bends when it passes through glass. Different kinds of glass have different refractive indexes.

DUST AND SOIL ANALYSIS

Because dust and soil are so easily carried from the crime scene – on skin, shoes, and clothing, or in the hair of a suspect – they are useful for comparison with similar substances at the scene. Both dust and soil vary greatly in their contents, often over a small area, so this analysis can prove quite accurate.

Crowbar used by a burglar to force open windows or doors

Wood chippings left at crime scene after chisel is used

Contents of vacuum cleaner bag from suspect's home may contain dust samples that match those at crime scene

Dust   Soil

Plastic bag thrown away in suspect's home may contain purchase receipt for items found at crime scene

WHAT RUBBISH!

Garbage is routinely searched for evidence after a crime. For example, discarded documents, such as letters, may reveal a suspect's movements in the weeks leading up to the crime. Search of a garbage pail may result in the recovery of actual evidence, such as a weapon or stained clothing.

LOOKING AT DOCUMENTS

No two people's handwriting is the same. A handwriting expert can compare a scribbled note to a handwriting sample from a suspect. A seemingly blank page may contain indents from writing on the previous page, which has been torn off. This, too, can be used to identify a suspect.

Chisel, used to force open a lock

IDENTIFYING TOOL MARKS

Marks are sometimes left by an implement, or tool, used to force open a door or window at a crime scene. Because the tool is harder than the wooden frame, it leaves an impressed imprint of its shape. Sometimes this can be matched to a tool owned by a suspect – particularly if it has a distinctive shape or marks of previous damage.

IN THE LABORATORY

Forensic laboratories usually specialize in one particular branch of science, such as biology, chemistry, or ballistics. Some of the equipment is specific to that subject, but most laboratories rely heavily on comparison microscopes (pp. 46–47). This busy laboratory (left), like most other labs, has evidence from hundreds of crimes awaiting analysis.

Fingerprints and DNA

Many early civilizations were aware of the unique nature of the ridges and furrows on the tips of the fingers. Chinese potters, for example, signed their work with a fingerprint. However, it was not until 1858 that William Herschel, an English civil servant in India, claimed that no two person's fingerprints are the same, and that they do not change with age. During the late 19th century, researchers developed a method of classifying prints so that they could be easily identified. Just as fingerprints are unique to an individual's fingertips, so deoxyribonucleic acid (DNA) is unique to every cell of an individual's body. In 1984, scientists began to create DNA profiles, sometimes called genetic fingerprints, from body fluids, flesh, skin, or hair roots. By matching the genetic information from a forensic sample with that of a suspect, investigators can prove a suspect guilty or innocent.

FRANCIS GALTON
Sir Francis Galton (1822–1911) was an English scientist who made the first advances in identifying the basic patterns of fingerprints. Sophisticated modern methods are based on the classification system he devised during the 19th century.

Roller to transfer ink to plate

Fingerprint ink

INK AND ROLL
The universal method of taking a suspect's fingerprints is called ink and roll. A thin coating of black ink is rolled onto a metal plate. Then, one by one, each of the subject's fingertips is rolled on the ink from one side of the nail to the other, then rolled onto a white chart, producing prints.

Lifting tape to remove prints from surface

Aluminum dusting powder, which reflects light and photographs well

BRUSHING UP
If fingerprints have been left in a substance such as blood or paint, they are easy to see. However, most prints are made by the oils and sweat on the surface of the skin and are almost invisible. The most common technique for revealing these fingerprints is to dust a fine powder over the surface, which sticks to the oily deposit. The powder-covered prints are removed from the surface on transparent sticky tape and then photographed. This officer is dusting for prints on a stolen car.

Fan-shaped brush for larger areas

Brush used with very fine powders

Long-handled brush for reaching into corners

Delicate "whisper" brush used with aluminum powder

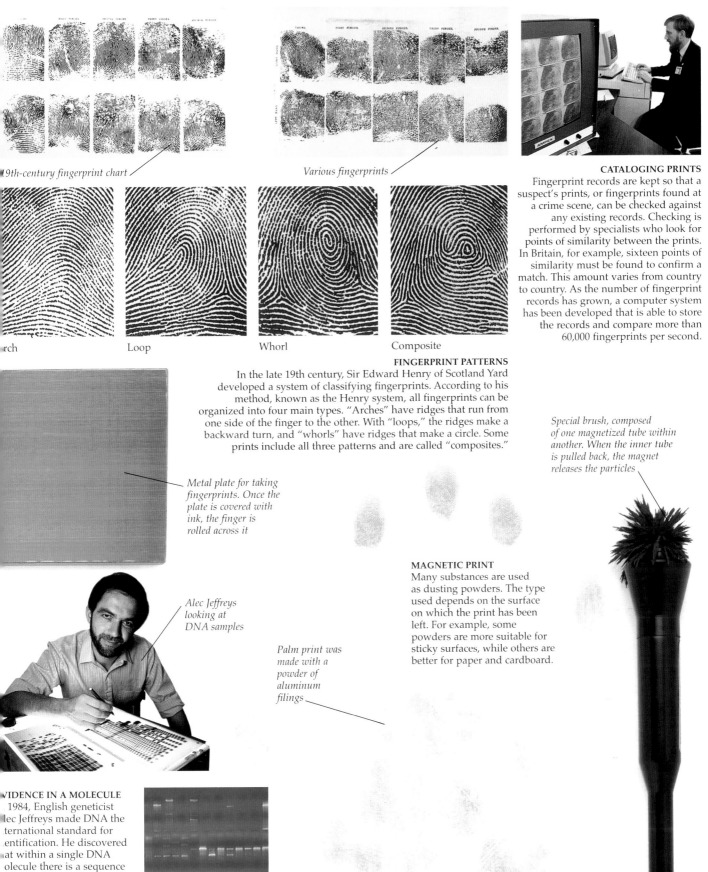

19th-century fingerprint chart

Various fingerprints

CATALOGING PRINTS
Fingerprint records are kept so that a suspect's prints, or fingerprints found at a crime scene, can be checked against any existing records. Checking is performed by specialists who look for points of similarity between the prints. In Britain, for example, sixteen points of similarity must be found to confirm a match. This amount varies from country to country. As the number of fingerprint records has grown, a computer system has been developed that is able to store the records and compare more than 60,000 fingerprints per second.

rch   Loop   Whorl   Composite

FINGERPRINT PATTERNS
In the late 19th century, Sir Edward Henry of Scotland Yard developed a system of classifying fingerprints. According to his method, known as the Henry system, all fingerprints can be organized into four main types. "Arches" have ridges that run from one side of the finger to the other. With "loops," the ridges make a backward turn, and "whorls" have ridges that make a circle. Some prints include all three patterns and are called "composites."

Special brush, composed of one magnetized tube within another. When the inner tube is pulled back, the magnet releases the particles

Metal plate for taking fingerprints. Once the plate is covered with ink, the finger is rolled across it

MAGNETIC PRINT
Many substances are used as dusting powders. The type used depends on the surface on which the print has been left. For example, some powders are more suitable for sticky surfaces, while others are better for paper and cardboard.

Alec Jeffreys looking at DNA samples

Palm print was made with a powder of aluminum filings

VIDENCE IN A MOLECULE
1984, English geneticist lec Jeffreys made DNA the ternational standard for entification. He discovered at within a single DNA olecule there is a sequence information unique to each dividual (except identical vins, who have the same NA). Like fingerprinting, NA profiling can be used connect a suspect with e scene of a crime.

BIOLOGICAL "PATTERN"
From a sample of any human tissue or body fluid, a biological "pattern" of that person can be created. This is called a DNA sample and looks like a supermarket bar code.

Forensic analysis

DESPITE DEVELOPMENTS IN technology, the basic principles of forensic science have remained the same. A forensic scientist's main task is comparison. For example, the scientist will compare a hair found at a crime scene with one from a suspect's head, or match a fabric fiber found in a suspect's car with the clothing worn by a victim. The main techniques used are microscopic examination and chemical analysis. A forensic laboratory will use several types of microscopes in their work; electron microscopes can magnify objects more than 150,000 times, which makes identification and comparison easier. Comparison microscopes are used, allowing a scientist to view two samples side by side through the eyepieces. Other types of microscope can help compare bullets to determine their source, or identify minerals and drugs. Forensic laboratory work combines many different disciplines, such as biology, chemistry, ballistics (the study of guns and ammunition), and document analysis.

Laser lamp used detect the presen of proteins, fou in body flui

NAPOLEON'S DEATH
Napoleon Bonaparte's death in 1821 was ascribed to stomach cancer. However, there have been persistent rumors that he was poisoned. In 1960, a forensic team analyzed a lock of Napoleon's hair taken from his head when he died. More than 13 times the normal level of arsenic was found. The poison could have been administered deliberately, or ingested by accident.

SEARCHING FOR SALIVA
Forensic scientists often look for evidence left at murder scenes. The pillow (above) has been sprayed with a substance that binds with protein. The protein will fluoresce under the laser lamp, showing the presence of body fluids, such as saliva. The pillow can then be sent to the laboratory for DNA analysis (pp. 44–45).

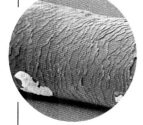

Human eyebrow magnified 500 times

Green cotton fibers and yellow polyester fibers magnified 1,000 times

Dog hairs magnified 1,000 times

Extracting solvent absorbs poisons as urine sample is spun

IN THE LABORATORY
The forensic laboratory is one of the most valuable tools in a crime investigation. Clothing, shoe prints (pp. 40–41), dust traces, weapons, and bullets are a few items that may be analyzed in the crime laboratory. This scientist is using a comparison microscope. Originally designed for the comparison of bullets and cartridge cases, it is now used to compare almost any kind of evidence. Two slides carrying samples are placed on the viewing tray. The slides are viewed simultaneously through the eyepieces.

Centrifuge spins at a rate of 2,000 to 3,000 revolutions per minute

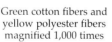

Scientist examines some fibers in an evidence bag under the microscope

IDENTIFYING POISONS

Thin-layer chromatography is a technique used to identify the various components in poison and drug samples extracted from body fluids. A glass slide is coated with silica gel, and spots of the sample are applied just above the bottom edge. The slide is lowered into a tank containing a liquid that reaches just below the line of sample spots. As the liquid rises up the gel (just as water rises through blotting paper), it carries with it the different components of the sample. As different substances rise at different rates, each sample is separated into a series of dots rising up the slide. Each dot is a different component of the sample. The slide can be compared with previous results and the components identified.

Left-hand column is a control. It is included as a guideline to help identify substances in the sample extracts

The control is made up of a mixture of three pure drugs. The middle one is methadone

Chromatogram of five sample extracts

This column is a sample from a drug abuser's urine. The highest spot is methadone

This spot shows there was nicotine in this sample

Shirt may smell of gasoline suggesting a possible cause of the fire

The arsonist's hair may be found on the shirt

SHIRT SLEEVE

This burned shirt sleeve, taken from the victim of a suspicious fire, will be sent to the laboratory. The autopsy had already proved the victim died before the fire started – there was no soot in the lungs, so he had not breathed smoke. Scientists will test the fabric to determine if it had an accelerant, such as gasoline, on it. Such a finding would strengthen the theory that the fire was started deliberately in an attempt to hide a murder.

SEPARATING SAMPLES

High-speed microcentrifuges are used to separate postmortem samples into their component parts. For example, an extracting solvent is added to a sample of blood in a test tube. The tube spins at high speed in the centrifuge. The solvent extracts any foreign substance, such as poison, from the blood. The lighter component (the poison absorbed in the solvent) rises to the top of the tube, while the heavier component (blood) sinks to the bottom. The solvent can then be tested to identify the poison.

Sample of stomach contents

Sample of urine

Sample of blood

MT97–56301

MT97–55233

BODY FLUID SAMPLES

If the postmortem examination of a body suggests poisoning, the pathologist sends samples of bodily fluids and parts of the vital organs to the laboratory for analysis. Tests will reveal whether the body contains poison, what the poison is, and how much of it is present.

The bare bones

F EW PEOPLE REALIZE HOW MUCH information an expert can glean from a pile of bones – information that can help solve a crime. Examination of a skeleton can reveal the gender of the deceased, as male and female skeletons have different skulls and pelvic (hip) bones. Even without a complete skeleton, height can be calculated within an inch (25 mm) by measuring the long bones (the femur in the leg or the tibia in the arm). Age can sometimes be determined from the way in which sections of the skull have closed together, or, up to the age of 25, from the development of the teeth. The structure of the head, face, teeth, and long bones can also indicate the indigenous group of the deceased.

MIKHAIL GERASIMO
Mikhail Gerasimov was a pioneer of faci reconstruction in Russia during the 195(The reconstruction of Tamerlane the Gre the Mongol king, was Gerasimov's greate achievement. In the illustration abov Gerasimov (left) and an archaeologi examine a 30,000-year-old skeleto

Cast of the skull, made of alginate

Work starts with the temples and the neck

Building the nose is very demanding

Wooden pegs

1 The skeleton of a young woman was dug up in Wales in 1989 and named "Little Miss Nobody" by the police. To begin the facial reconstruction, a cast of the skull is made. Then pegs are inserted at fixed points to indicate the standard thickness of the flesh.

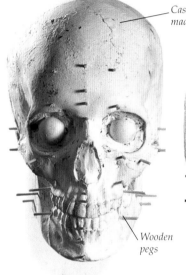

A male sacrum is narrower than a female sacrum

2 Plastic balls make "eyes" and the "flesh" is built up in clay. With the shape of the skull and the length of the pegs as guides, the muscles of the face begin to form.

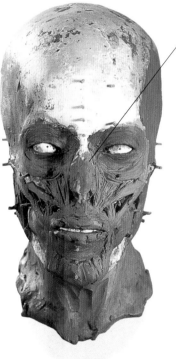

3 After the mouth, the areas around the eye sockets are carefully filled in. Then the nose is formed. Because there are few bones that indicate the shape of the nose, this is one of the most difficult parts of the reconstruction.

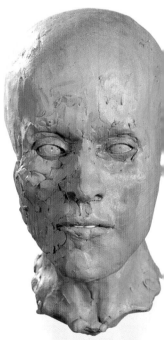

4 The clay has now been filled o to the tops of the guide pegs and the sculptor is ready to put th finishing touches on the head. All that remains is to smooth the surface to give a more lifelike appearance. If the age of the person at death is known, the sculptor can texture the skin correctly. The whole process takes little more than a day to complete.

HIS AND HERS
Men and women have different skeletons. Male skulls have a little lump at the back of the head called the nuchal crest and another on the forehead called the suborbital ridge. The sciatic notch on the hips is wider on the female skeleton than on the male. The sacrum, at the bottom of the spine, is smaller in males than females.

LASER RECONSTRUCTION
The use of laser technology in the re-creation of faces was pioneered by forensic pathologist Dr. Peter Vanezis, seen here demonstrating a new system in London, England. When Karen Price was identified, Dr. Vanezis used a laser technique to superimpose a photograph on the skull made by Richard Neave. They fitted perfectly.

THE FACE MAKER
Richard Neave is a medical illustrator from Manchester University in England. Although Neave's early work was with archaeological remains – he rebuilt the head of King Midas – he has recently worked with the police on building the faces of murder and accident victims. Neave is seen here working on the skull of Karen Price.

Although just a guess, Karen's hairstyle proved quite accurate

*oen if the hair length is
nown, it is impossible
to tell the style*

*xperience and
stinct enable the
ulptor to reconstruct
e soft tissues of the
se, lips, and ears*

*he sinews of the neck
n be determined
om the bone
ructure*

5 Photographs of the facial reconstruction were published in police notices and newspapers, and broadcast on television. As a result, a name was put to the anonymous skeleton. She was identified as Karen Price by a Cardiff social worker. Later, two men were charged with Karen's murder.

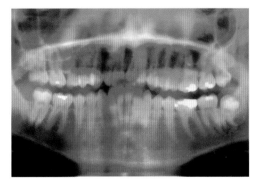

DENTAL IDENTIFICATION
Because teeth are almost indestructible, they can often be used to identify a body when other methods cannot (for example, following a fire or an air crash). A panoramic photograph, like this one, is taken of the surviving teeth and matched to the victim's dental record. As no two people have identical dental histories, this method is accurate.

Attention to detail

THERE ARE FEW "OPEN AND SHUT" cases – crimes where it is known immediately what happened, who did it, and why. Investigators usually put together a case from lots of small clues. Often no detail is too insignificant. A witness may remember the color or make of a car, or even its license plate number. An onlooker may have noticed something about a suspect – his or her voice, a physical feature, or a distinctive tattoo. Sometimes a witness recalls the criminal's distinctive clothing or jewelry. These eyewitness details are added to the other clues picked up by scene-of-crime officers and forensic scientists and built into a case to be presented later in court.

LINE
Lineups are used by police throughout most of t world. A suspect takes any position in a line of oth people of similar appearance. The witness is th asked to identify the suspect. Lineups are not alwa reliable. If the real criminal is not there, a witness m choose the person who looks most like the crimin

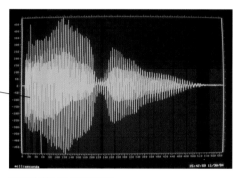

This "bar print" represents the sound made by a person saying the word baby

DISTINGUISHING MARKS
Members of gangs often like to have some way of identifying fellow members. Tattoos are a good means of identification because they cannot easily be erased. Tattoos are used by members of Chinese secret societies, such as the Triads. Individually chosen tattoos are even more useful to the police, because no two people are likely to carry the same pattern of markings.

Death's head (skull) rings are popular with motorcycle gangs

VOICE RECOGNITION
Each human voice has a unique "print." The current system of recording and identifying voiceprints was developed during World War II. In the bar print above, the horizontal axis records the length of time, the vertical axis measures the strength of the sound. Voiceprints can be used to identify a suspect in cases of abusive telephone calls or demands for ransom payments made by phone.

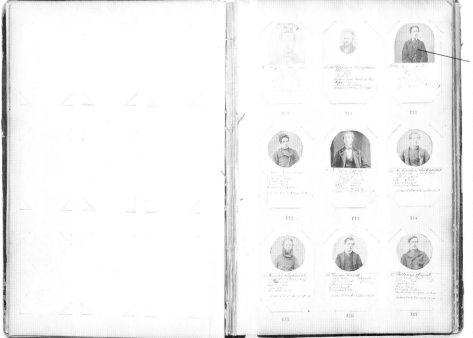

Photographic strips of eyes

Photographic strips of noses

A 19th-century mug shot

"MUG SHOT" BOOK
After photography's invention in the mid-19th century, one of its most important uses was to allow police to keep visual as well as written records of criminals. This is one of the earliest examples of a mug shot book, from the City of London Police. At that time, similar records were being kept in the United States, under the direction of Thomas Byrnes of the New York Police. In France, Alphonse Bertillon (pp. 52–53) was improving the French system by photographing criminals.

COMPUTER-AIDED VIDEO-FIT

Improved computer technology has led to the videofit, which replaces Photo-fit identification. Above, a witness is selecting the general hairstyle of the suspect. This choice is transferred to the video screen, where it can be altered to give a closer likeness. Another recent development makes the video-fit three-dimensional so that it can be seen and altered at different angles.

LICENSE PLATES

All countries have a system of matching vehicles to their owners. This information can be used by the police to check whether a vehicle has been stolen or reported at a crime scene, and to find out about the owner. Many criminals put false plates on cars to avoid detection. The British plate above is false. The numbers are too small and thick, making them difficult to read. The middle plate is a temporary French plate. The letters *WW* show it was issued to a person moving to a new home.

False British plate

Temporary French plate

4269 WWE 75
RENAULT COLISEUM PARIS 9ᵉ ☎ 45.26.87.89

German export plate

HH-936 W 96/9
HONDA Autohaus Elbgemeinden · 2000 Schenefeld ☎ 8 30 60 80

These numbers indicate that the vehicle should have left the country by September 1996

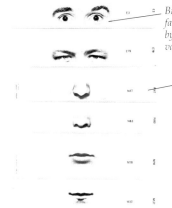

Billions of different faces can be made by combining various strips

One strip that will make the nose of a Photo-fit

SELECTING EACH FEATURE

This selection of just two pairs of eyes, two noses, and two mouths from a Penry Photo-fit kit shows how much features can differ. The kits have about 100 different eyes, noses, and mouths. This collection represents only a small proportion of the huge variety that exists in people's features. Unlike the video-fit, Photo-fit just gives the "feeling" or "look" of a person, rather than a close representation.

A photographic strip of someone's hairline

The Photo-fit

The original subject

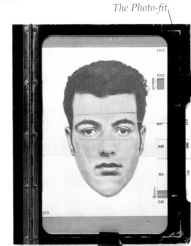

PHOTO-FIT CASE

In 1971, Britain introduced the Penry Facial Identification Technique (Photo-fit). British forensic scientist Jacques Penry's kit consisted of photographic strips of different eyes, noses, mouths, jaw lines, hairlines, and ears. These features were put together by the crime witness and a police expert. The resulting Photo-fit was circulated, often leading to a conviction.

MAKING UP A FACE

To demonstrate the Photo-fit method, a "witness" was shown an ordinary member of the public (above right) and then asked to construct the portrait (above left) from memory. In a real crime situation, a traumatized witness may not remember the exact appearance of a criminal. For this reason, eyewitness identification has become devalued.

Criminal characteristics

FOR HUNDREDS OF YEARS scientists have investigated the theory that certain people are born to be criminals. In the mid-19th century, anthropology, the study of humankind, became a popular science. Anthropologists studying the field of abnormal behavior examined various types of criminals to see if they shared any physical characteristics. One of the early researchers was a French prison doctor named Lauvergne, who made plaster casts of his patients' heads to demonstrate their "evil" features. Most of Lauvergne's work was found to be incorrect. However, at the same time, Alphonse Bertillon, working for the Paris police force, was also taking detailed measurements of criminals' heads and bodies, but for a different purpose. He was using the measurements to identify known criminals, rather than to create a physical profile of a criminal type.

"SHERLOCK HOLMES OF THE COUCH
Dr. James Brussel, an American crimin psychiatrist, has been called "the Sherloc Holmes of the couch." Brussel was pioneer in psychiatric profiling – method of deducing a criminal characteristics by studying the way crime is carried out. Dr. Brussel use his theory successfully to help sol many crimes. He helped captu New York's "Mad Bomber" 1957 (below) and helped cato Albert DeSalvo, the "Bosto Strangler," in 196

WITCH HUNTS
In medieval times, it was thought that all witches had certain characteristics, such as warts or moles. Women thought to be witches were subjected to the ducking chair – being immersed in water while tied into a chair. If they did not drown, it was thought to prove they were witches, and they were executed anyway.

According to Gall, the brain is divided into seven main sections, each with a specific purpose (for example, intellectual or domestic)

Within each brain section, there are several areas that represent different functions, such as friendship and courage

PHRENOLOGY
In 1796, Dr. Franz Gall, a doctor in Vienna, announced his theory of phrenology, in which a person's qualities and abilities are traced to particular areas of the brain. Gall believed that while people thought, their brains and skulls changed shape, causing bumps on the surface. Phrenologists thought a person's character could be understood by studying the shape of the skull. This pseudoscience was initially popular, but was soon rejected as false.

THE MAD BOMBE
In 1940, George Metesky began a 16-ye series of bombings to seek revenge on h previous employer, who he believe had wronged him. The accurate descriptio of Metesky given by Dr. James Brussel led Metesky's arrest (above). Metesky was four unfit to stand trial and was committed to state hospital for the criminally insan

CESARE LOMBROSO
An Italian psychiatrist of the mid-19th century, Cesare Lombroso made a study of 7,000 criminals in order to prove that different "criminal types" could be identified by physical characteristics. For example, he believed that swindlers and bandits had larger-than-normal heads, and that thieves and highwaymen had thick hair and beards. He never proved his theories despite the elaborate instruments he invented in order to do so.

Double-headed calipers for smaller measurements

ALPHONSE BERTILLON

Bertillon was an assistant clerk in the records office of the Judicial Identification Service in the Paris police force when, in 1883, he proposed his theory of anthropometry ("man measurement"). Bertillon concluded that no two human beings have exactly the same measurements, and he devised a method of identifying criminals by comparing records of individual physical attributes. Bertillonage was adopted as a general system in France. However, it was soon replaced by fingerprinting (pp. 44–45).

MEASURING GAUGES

Bertillon's father was a doctor and had a room full of scientific instruments for measuring the body. The younger Bertillon found these instruments fascinating. When he began to experiment for himself, he collected his own set of calipers and gauges, which he later used to test his theory of anthropometry. These gauges, right, and calipers, left, are the types Bertillon used.

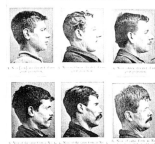

Original Bertillon "mug shot" book

Gauge for larger measurements

BOOK OF FEATURES

Another of Alphonse Bertillon's successes was recognizing the value of the newly invented science of photography. Prior to this, the visual appearance of criminals was recorded in words, called a *portrait parlé*, or spoken picture. It became possible to assemble classified books of photographic portraits. Looking at these, witnesses could identify criminals These are the predecessors of mug-shot books, commonly used today.

Measurements of suspects are taken in the Bertillonage room of the police headquarters

Photographs of the criminal from the front and side

CRIMINAL RECORD

Bertillon's clerks kept detailed files that included names, addresses, and crimes committed. Also recorded were various measurements of parts of the body. Eventually, photographs of the criminal, including both front and side views, were attached. This method of presenting full-face and profile shots is now used throughout the world.

BERTILLONAGE AT WORK

Within three months of proving his theory of anthropometry, Bertillon used his method to convict a thief named Dupont. Dupont had been brought to the police station, on a charge of theft. Bertillon measured him and recognized the results. Dupont had been convicted of theft before and measured by Bertillon. However, during the first arrest, Dupont was using a different false name. Bertillon's method proved it was the same person, and this was enough to convict him a second time.

An elaborate kind of a ruler for measuring smaller parts of the body, such as fingers

Following a scent

DOGS HAVE A SUPERIOR SENSE OF SMELL to humans, and their keen noses have made them useful colleagues in the police fight against crime. By following an individual's unique and invisible scent, dogs are able to track down his or her whereabouts. Police forces train dogs to chase, grab, and hold a suspect, and then release the suspect on command. Dogs have been used to track criminals for a long time. References to police dogs can be found in the 19th-century writings of Charles Dickens and Sir Arthur Conan Doyle, and in the 19th-century United States, dogs were often used to hunt escaped convicts and runaway slaves. During the 20th century, the role of the canine detective has grown. Police and other law enforcement agencies now train dogs to sniff out drugs and explosives.

BLOODHOUNDS
Traditionally, tracking human beings has been the bloodhound's special skill. Commissioner Sir Charles Warren introduced bloodhounds to London's Metropolitan Police in the 1880s. To test the bloodhounds' ability, Sir Charles acted as quarry to see if the dogs could track him down. They did – and one of them bit him! However, bloodhounds have now been replaced by lighter, more agile breeds.

CHECKING A CAR
Many vehicles travel around the world on ships and ferries. At ports, specially trained sniffer dogs inspect vehicles for illegal substances such as drugs. Here, a dog is checking the engine compartment of a car.

SUSPICIOUS SUITCASE
Airports also face smuggling problems. Dogs are used to search baggage holds. They are trained to recognize and detect the scents of contraband items such as drugs or bomb-making equipment. The dog alerts its handler if it picks up a suspicious scent.

Most popular police dog breed is the German shepherd

SPECIAL TRAINING
Only puppies with good temperaments are selected for the rigorous training that a police dog must complete. A 14-week-old puppy is given to a handler, who takes it home to become part of his or her family. When the dog is one year old, it receives 14 weeks of basic training, during which it is taught to obey voice and hand signals and to track and hold a fugitive. The training also involves fitness exercises to build the dog's stamina and agility.

SUPER SENSE
All around the world customs and excise authorities (pp. 28–29) use dogs to sniff out illicit chemicals. Springer and cocker spaniels and Labrador retrievers are commonly used to hunt out substances such as cocaine and marijuana. However, sniffer dogs hunt not only for drugs. The U.S. Department of Agriculture has its own "Beagle Brigade" to search for illicit fruit and meat in airports.

Springer spaniel wears reflector harness when working in restricted light

REX III
Perhaps the best-known of all police dogs was Rex III, whose exploits in England during the 1950s are almost legendary, Rex III made more than 130 "arrests" and was the first dog to work with the famous Flying Squad and to be trained to detect drugs. During his active service, Rex III was awarded many honors and medals.

FINDING A VICTIM
During the blitz of London in World War II, sniffer dogs were used to locate people buried beneath the debris of bombed buildings. Dogs are also used in murder investigations to locate the victims' bodies.

Camera and lights

Harness is specially designed to be comfortable and lightweight

ON THE TRAIL OF A SUSPECT
Like police horses (pp. 34–35), dogs are trained to ignore loud noises such as gunfire. During their training, police dogs are taught the best way to attack and to avoid being clubbed by a weapon. Sadly, many brave animals are still killed in the line of duty.

Battery pack to power lights and camera

LIGHTS, CAMERA, ACTION
Besides their superior sense of smell, sniffer dogs have another advantage over humans – they can search very small spaces. This dog is going to search a small area on the other side of a trapdoor. The animal is fitted with a special harness that contains a small video camera, lights, and a battery pack. This allows the handler to see the interior area.

Instructor wears protective padding

ARRESTED BY A DOG
Police dogs are taught to attack a suspect only on the command of their handler. During their training, police dogs learn how to restrain a suspect by the arm. An instructor, wearing heavily padded sleeves to prevent injury, plays the part of the fleeing suspect. Despite their efficiency when attacking, police dogs have gentle natures.

Dog practises attacking many times during training

Outlaws

IT IS A STRANGE FACT that some of the worst criminals in history have become popular folk heroes. One of the best examples is Dick Turpin (p. 14), a murderous thug who terrorized travelers in the countryside around London during the 18th century. He became a romantic figure after the publication of *Rookwood* (1834), a novel written by Henry Ainsworth in which Turpin was portrayed as a chivalrous highwayman riding his trusty horse, Black Bess. Books are not the only inspiration for hero worship. Some people long for the freedom of an outlaw, and admire his or her daring. More recent antiheroes range from the Great Train Robbers (p. 17) to India's Bandit Queen (below).

ROBIN HOOD
England's most legendary outlaw, Robin Hood, robbed the rich and gave to the poor. There is no evidence that he actually existed; the stories of Robin's adventures are based on medieval ballads that have been embellished through the centuries. He has remained popular and has become the subject of numerous films, such as *The Adventures of Robin Hood* (above), 1938, starring Errol Flynn as the notorious outlaw.

LOUIS MANDRIN
Louis Mandrin was one of the best-loved smugglers France has ever known. In the 1740s, he formed a gang of 2,000 men, who were so well trained that they often defeated the king's troops. Mandrin's dashing adventures made him the people's hero. He was captured in 1755 and was executed by being tied to a large wheel. His limbs were crushed as the wheel turned, and he was left to die.

BUTCH AND SUNDANCE
Butch Cassidy and the Sundance Kid were members of the outlaw gang the Wild Bunch, who operated during the 1890s in the western United States. From their hideout, the Hole in the Wall, they specialized in large-scale horse and cattle rustling and armed robberies of banks and trains. These outlaw gangs were always popular with the public, but Butch and Sundance became particularly well known after a romanticized film was made in 1969 (right).

In the 1969 film Butch Cassidy and the Sundance Kid, *Butch was played by actor Paul Newman*

The Sundance Kid was played by actor Robert Redford

A film has been made, called Bandit Queen, *about Phoolan Devi*

THE BANDIT QUEEN
Phoolan Devi, also known as the Bandit Queen, was imprisoned in 1983 in India for banditry and murder. A rebel against her fate as a low-caste woman, Devi became a heroine to thousands of Indians. Once released, she fought politically for women's rights.

Butch Cassidy's real name was Robert LeRoy Parker

Sundance's real name was Harry Longbaugh

Bonnie Parker's body armor, found on the ground near the car in which she and Clyde were shot

The back of Bonnie Parker's body armor

Bonnie and Clyde had removed their body armor while they ate lunch

A bullet hole made during the final shoot-out

ody armor ade of bullet-roof material

Floyd Hamilton's rifle

BEFORE THEY MET
Clyde Barrow was born into a poor Texas family in 1909. He was already under arrest for robbery when he met Bonnie Parker. She came from a more respectable family, had married and been left when, at the age of 19, she met Clyde. In 1932, the pair began their dramatic but short-lived partnership.

Clyde's watch

Miniature boots made by Clyde Barrow for his mother

hotographs of lanche Barrow

lanche wrote f her advancing lindess in later ears on the back f this photograph

BONNIE AND CLYDE
In 1932, Clyde Barrow and Bonnie Parker teamed up to become the most infamous pair of robbers and murderers of the decade. They terrorized the southwestern United States, murdering at least 13 people. In 1934, Bonnie and Clyde were ambushed by police officers, who killed them by firing 150 gunshots into their car.

GANG MEMBERS
Clyde's brother Buck and sister-in-law Blanche were also members of the gang along with robber Floyd Hamilton. Buck was shot dead in 1933, while Blanche was captured and imprisoned. In 1938, Hamilton was sentenced to 20 years in Alcatraz (pp. 12–13).

A WANTED poster put out for Bonnie and Clyde

Strange but true

CRIME AND THE LAW are serious subjects. However, crime also has its share of lighter moments and strange stories. Sometimes criminals are just foolish – such as armed robber José Sanchez. In 1995, when police arrived at the scene of an armed robbery in New Jersey, they found a piece of paper that the robber had used to wedge open the door of the building. It turned out to be a traffic ticket issued to Sanchez the night before the robbery, and it had his name and home address printed on it. There are other crimes that are strange because of the daring or ingenuity of the criminals, or because of the motives that inspired them. For example, in 1981 John Hinckley attempted to assassinate President Ronald Reagan in an effort to impress actress Jodie Foster, with whom Hinckley was obsessed.

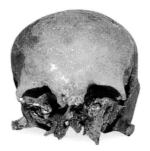

LINDOW WOMAN
In 1983, a badly decomposed female head was dug up at Lindow Moss in Cheshire, England. Frightened by the discovery, a local man confessed to the police that he had killed his wife 23 years before and buried her in the peat bog. In fact, when the remains were scientifically dated, they were found to be more than 1,770 years old.

ON BOTH SIDES OF THE LAW
Welshman Henry Morgan was a famous buccaneer in the Caribbean of the 17th century. With the unofficial support of the English government, he spent over 10 years attacking Dutch and Spanish colonies in the area. In 1670, Morgan raided Spanish-owned Panama. Because the raid took place after a peace treaty between England and Spain, he was arrested, transported to London, and charged with piracy. Relations with Spain soured, and King Charles II pardoned and knighted Morgan, then sent him back to Jamaica as deputy governor.

AVENGING "NAILS" MORTON'S DEATH
Dion O'Banion (above) was one of Chicago's most notorious gangsters, and Samuel "Nails" Morton was his most loyal gunman. Morton had been awarded the Croix de Guerre during active service in World War I and was considered indestructible. However, Morton was thrown by a horse and killed while riding in Lincoln Park. In revenge, O'Banion sent gunmen to kill the horse.

Tilh was tried, found guilty, and hanged

Jodie Foster and Richard Gere starred in the 1993 film Sommersby, *which was loosely based on the story of Martin Guerre*

FAKE IDENTITY
After having disappeared for eight years, Martin Guerre returned in 1556 to his home in the French village of Artigat. He was welcomed by all except his uncle, who insisted that this Martin was an impostor. Guerre's uncle was right. Arnaud du Tilh had met Guerre, got a detailed picture of his life, and adopted his identity. Tilh almost got away with it – until the real Martin Guerre came back.

MURDERING THE PRESIDENT
In 1963, President John F. Kennedy was assassinated in Dallas, Texas. Lee Harvey Oswald was arrested for the crime. However, because it was not a federal crime to murder the president, neither the FBI nor the Secret Service could take Oswald into custody. Instead, he was taken to a Dallas county jail, where, because of lapses in security, he was shot dead before he could be put on trial.

J.S.G. Boggs's drawing of an English five-pound note

FORGER OR ARTIST

In October 1986, J.S.G. Boggs, an American artist, was showing his work at London's Young Unknowns Gallery. To everyone's surprise, the police arrived and seized the pieces, which were drawings of English bank notes. The Bank of England prosecuted under the Forgery and Counterfeiting Act, but Boggs was acquitted.

ESCAPE FROM THE COURTROOM

On the night of July 17, 1976, Albert Spaggiari robbed the bank Société Générale in Nice, France, after breaking in through the underground sewer system. Spaggiari was captured and put on trial for his crime, but he made a dramatic leap from the dock and slipped out through a window. During his 12 years on the run, Spaggiari hid behind homemade disguises like the one above.

BUTTERFLY LAW

Most countries have rules about killing certain species of wildlife. In California, there is a law intended to protect butterflies. City Ordinance Number 352 in Pacific Grove makes it a misdemeanor to "kill or threaten a butterfly," such as the swallowtail above.

J.S.G. Boggs holding some of his drawings of bank notes

Italian, U.S., and English currency

INTERNET SWEET-SHOP

A 15-year-old boy from Dublin, Ireland, used his parents' computer to order candy from a U.S. company via the Internet. When the company asked for a credit card number, the boy simply made one up. Unfortunately, it was the real account number of someone in Argentina, and $2,000 worth of chocolate arrived at the boy's home. Since the culprit was a juvenile, he was not charged.

"TITANIC" THOMPSON

In April 1912, when the liner *Titanic* struck an iceberg off Newfoundland, 1,513 lives were lost. One who did not perish was Alvon Clarence Thompson. Since women and children had priority in the escape, Thompson dressed as a woman to make sure of a place in a lifeboat. After his return to the United States, Thompson began to collect on the insurance policies of the *Titanic*'s victims, whom he claimed as relatives.

Did you know?

AMAZING FACTS

The fictional detective Sherlock Holmes has one of the most famous addresses in all of literature: 221 B Baker Street, London. Although Baker Street exists, there was no number 221 during the years Holmes solved mysteries. Today, the building at number 221 is one of the London offices for the Abbey Building Society (a type of bank). The English Heritage Organization has posted a blue plaque on the building's facade to mark it as the former home of an important public figure. Someone is employed by the bank to answer the hundreds of letters and cards that come addressed to Sherlock Holmes every year from around the world.

THE SHERLOCK HOLMES MUSEUM

221B BAKER ST

SHERLOCK HOLMES

Consulting Detective

1881 - 1904

HERITAGE PLAQUE

Baker Street plaque

Footprints do not only reveal what type of shoes a suspect was wearing. They can also give clues about the suspect's weight, height, likely age, which direction he was moving in, how fast he was going, and even if he was holding anything as he moved.

A single strand of hair can provide plenty of information to skilled investigators. They can determine whether the hair was pulled out or cut, whether the hair came from an animal or a person, and what part of the body the hair is from. It is not possible to tell whether hair came from a male or female, however, unless the root of the hair is still attached, providing DNA, which can indicate gender.

An investigator collects evidence.

Whenever someone is in a room, they leave a trace of themselves behind, whether it is saliva on a chewed pencil top or a tiny flake of skin. Forensic investigators use special vacuum cleaners that concentrate that kind of evidence onto an evidence pad; the pad is then examined for cells.

Can a skeleton provide the key to solving a crime? A human skeleton provides many clues for a crime investigator. The bone structure (particularly the pelvic bone) can determine gender. Disease and illness can leave evidence in the bones, so an investigator can work out whether or not the person was healthy. The bones even give clues about the person's occupation (heavy labor, for example, leaves certain changes in bone structure) and where a person may have lived, by means of a chemical analysis.

A trail of footprints

The first recorded reference to forensics may have been in a Chinese book written in 1428. The book told how to tell the difference between someone who had drowned and someone who had been strangled.

A forensic entomologist (a scientist who studies insects) determines the length of time a body has been dead (or if it has been moved) by studying arthropods found on human remains. Arthropods feed on dead vertebrates and have a consistent life cycle, helping pinpoint the time of death.

Blood makes up less than 10 percent of a healthy person's body weight, but when it is spilled, a little goes a long way. It is very difficult for a criminal to clean up all traces of blood at a crime scene, as it can adhere to his clothing or the murder weapon easily. Forensic serologists (experts on blood) can derive a great deal of evidence from a tiny amount of blood.

In 1902, prison wardens routinely took fingerprint records of convicts, but the first person to be convicted of a crime on fingerprint evidence was British criminal Henry Jackson. Jackson's grubby fingerprints were found on the window of a house that had just been burglarized; Jackson, who had stolen some billiard balls, left his mark on the window as he escaped from it. His prints were matched to those on file with his former prison warden, and Jackson was convicted.

In theory, any ridged body part can be used as a means of identification, although the police do not keep files of every body part. Toe prints, footprints, palm prints, and even lip prints have all provided investigators with evidence.

In the past, some criminals went to wild extremes to prevent leaving fingerprint evidence. American gangster John Dillinger had his fingertips treated with acid to remove the ridge patterns (they grew back). Criminal Robert Phillips had the skin on his fingertips removed by plastic surgery, and replaced with skin grafts taken from his chest. Phillips was caught based on ridge evidence from the undoctored lower parts of his fingers.

Most of us are familiar with the use of dental records in identifying a body. Teeth decay far more slowly than bones, and can withstand burning in a fire. People who visited the dentist frequently and have had many dental treatments are easiest to identify. If the subject has no teeth, studying dentures and x-raying the mouth and skull can provide some evidence.

Every time a gun is fired, it leaves behind identical marks on the bullets and cartridge casings. No two guns leave the same marks; they are as unique as human fingerprints. These ballistic fingerprints help law enforcement agencies solve gun crimes by identifying the specific weapon used in a crime.

Looking at the way blood drops and splashes helps police determine the positions of the victim and criminal at the time of an assault.

Fired bullets

QUESTIONS AND ANSWERS

Q What is identity theft? Where can I get advice on preventing it?

A Identity theft may be the fastest-growing crime in the world. It is defined as the adoption of a person's identity for financial gain, or to aid in committing a crime. Identity thieves often open new credit card accounts and run up huge bills, or access bank accounts and empty them of funds. The Federal Trade Commission Web site (www.ftc.gov) has tips to help you protect your identity.

Q How does retinal scanning work?

A Retinal scanning analyzes the layer of blood vessels at the back of the eye. The scanning device uses a low-intensity light and an optical coupler to read the patterns. The user looks through a small opening in the scanner and focuses on a small green light for several seconds; the pattern is matched with one already on file to verify identity. As early as the 1930s, scientists discovered that these patterns were unique to each individual, but it took some time for technology to catch up. The first scan device for commercial use was introduced in 1984.

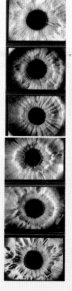

Retinal scans

Q What is luminol, and how do crime scene investigators use it?

A Sometimes at a crime scene, the blood has been washed away. How do investigators find out where it was? They spray the area with a chemical called luminol. This chemical reacts to hemoglobin (the oxygen-carrying protein in red blood cells), glowing greenish blue when it comes into contact with traces of blood. Investigators usually dim the lights so the glow is easy to see, then spray the chemical over a wide area and photograph or videotape the result.

Q What is computer forensics, and why is it important?

A The analysis of home computers and computer servers to determine if the computer has been used for illegal (or suspicious) activities is called computer forensics. It is becoming an important key in cracking criminal cases, since anything that helps police build up a picture of a suspect's interests and circle of contacts before the crime was committed is very useful.

Q How can investigators make sure they find as many fingerprints as they can at a crime scene?

A One everyday substance helps lift fingerprints from previously stubborn surfaces such as mirrors, plastic bags, or car windows: super glue. A chemical in the glue called cyanoacrylate is attracted to the fats and proteins left behind by a human touch. The item to be checked for fingerprints is put in a sealed tank. The glue is heated in a metal cup inside the tank. The glue vapor attaches itself to any fats and proteins, leaving behind a record of the fingerprint.

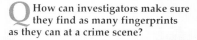

Fingerprint

Q Are lie detector tests accurate?

A The polygraph, or lie detector, is a machine that measures changes in the breathing rate, blood pressure, and perspiration of a crime suspect. The suspect is hooked up to the machine and asked to answer questions, including those with known answers such as age and sex. The person administering the test looks for changes in body responses when the subject tells the truth—and when he or she does not! The test results are not accepted as evidence in court unless a judge allows it. Scientists are working on more accurate methods, such as voice analyzers that look for the tremors in speech that appear when a person lies.

Q What is mass spectrometry, and how is it changing the field of forensics?

A A machine called a mass spectrometer identifies forensic samples, such as blood or explosives, by examining their molecular mass. Tiny droplets of water are sprayed at the sample, dislodging some of its molecules, which are sucked into the spectrometer for analysis. In 2004, scientists at Purdue University created a portable spectrometer. This machine could be taken to a crime scene and used on the spot, with no need to send evidence off to a lab for analysis.

Q What is psychological profiling? How is it used?

A In the 1950s, psychologists began to study common behavior patterns and personality traits in criminals. Police worked with these experts to determine the type of person who may have committed a particular crime. In the 1970s, the FBI established a Behavioral Science Unit where profilers examined crime cases, looking for details that might provide clues about a criminal's background and motivation. A profile includes general information such as the age or sex of the criminal, as well as specific details.

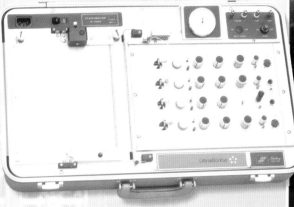

Polygraph

Record Breakers

LONGEST CRIMINAL TRIAL IN THE U.S.
The McMartin trial, which tried seven owners and teachers of a Caliornia preschool on charges of abuse, was the longest (1984–1990) and costliest ($13.2 million dollars) trial so far on record.

BIGGEST HEIST IN HISTORY
Gold, currency, and jewels worth an estimated $2.5 billion dollars were snatched in the German Riechsbank robbery in 1945.

LARGEST ART THEFT IN US HISTORY
In 1990, a dozen paintings, collectively worth $100 million dollars, were stolen from the Isabella Stewart Gardner Museum in Boston, MA.

LARGEST JEWEL HEIST
A 2003 raid on high-security vaults at the Diamond Center in Antwerp, Belgium, netted more than $100 million in jewels, gold, and securities.

BIGGEST CASH HEIST
A gang of thieves made off with at least $39 million dollars in cash from the vaults of a bank in Belfast, Northern Ireland, in 2004.

Timeline

SO MUCH TIME—SO MUCH CRIME! Ever since the first laws were laid down in ancient times, there were people willing to break them. This timeline provides a look at some of the most gripping crimes in history. You will learn about the world's infamous criminals and super sleuths, as well as the developments in detection that have helped crime-stoppers solve criminal cases.

Painting of Moses

c. 1750 BCE

King Hammurabi of Babylon issues a legal code, the first written code of laws yet discovered. The code contains 281 laws, including the well-known rules, "an eye for an eye" and "a tooth for a tooth."

c. 1200 BCE

According to the Old Testament, the prophet Moses receives the Ten Commandments from God. These divine laws have an important place in the ethical systems of Judaism, Christianity, and Islam.

621 BCE

The Greek ruler Draco creates notoriously harsh codes of law; most crimes are punishable by death.

c. CE 200

The Mishnah, the first recording of Judaism's oral laws, is compiled.

534

Roman Emperor Justinian collects all existing Roman laws into a simple and clear system of laws. His work is known as the Justinian Code.

c. 570

The prophet Muhammad, founder of Islam, is born in Saudi Arabia. Muslims believe that God revealed laws to him that form the basis of Islamic faith and law.

1110

The White Tower is completed at the Tower of London, England. The Tower serves as a prison and place of execution; famous prisoners over the years includes Sir Walter Raleigh, Ann Boleyn, and Guy Fawkes.

1382

Construction ends on the Bastille, built to defend the eastern part of Paris, France; this stronghold later becomes a prison.

1605

English soldier Guy Fawkes is caught making a huge bomb underneath the Houses of Parliament in London, England. He was executed for conspiring to kill the king and members of Parliament.

1667

The first French police force is founded by Marquis de Louvois and Gabriel La Reynie.

1671

Disguised as a parson, the Irish rogue Thomas Blood attempts to steal England's Crown Jewels. He is arrested with a crown, orb, and scepter.

1716–1718

British pirate Blackbeard (whose real name was thought to be Edward Teach) and his crew terrorize sailors on the Atlantic Ocean and the Caribbean Sea.

1787

Great Britain begins transporting prisoners to Australia.

1789

A crowd in Paris, France, storms the Bastille, releasing the prisoners, marking the beginning of the French Revolution.

1829

The Metropolitan Police Act, proposed by Sir Robert Peel, establishes police force in London at Scotland Yard. Officers are nicknamed "bobbies" after Peel.

Canadian "Mountie"

1848

U.S. lawman and gambler Wyatt Earp is born.

1852

The Pinkerton Detective Agency is founded in Chicago. Its logo was an open eye with the words, "We never sleep." This is the origin of the term, private eye.

Wyatt Earp

1873

The Canadian government forms the North-West Mounted Police (popularly known as "Mounties").

1873

The notorious James brothers, Jesse (1847–1882) and Frank (1843–1915), lead a gang of bandits in their first train robbery.

1881

American outlaw Billy the Kid (c. 1859–1881) is hunted down and shot by Sheriff Pat Garrett.

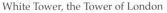

White Tower, the Tower of London

1888

Jack the Ripper terrorizes London, England. He kills seven women but eludes capture.

1892

Sir Francis Galton publishes his book on fingerprinting, significantly advancing the science of fingerprint identification.

1893

A U.S. court finds Lizzie Borden (1860–1927) not guilty of killing her parents with an axe. Her trial inspires a popular schoolyard chant.

Engraving of Jack the Ripper with a potential victim

1896

Wild West outlaw Butch Cassidy (1866–c. 1909) forms the Wild Bunch, a league of train robbers.

1908

The Siberian mystic Rasputin (1869–1916) heals the sick son of the Russian czar and gains power over the Imperial Family; he is murdered in 1916 by other royals.

1908

The Federal Bureau of Investigation (FBI) is created in the United States.

1909 MI5

Originally called the Special Intelligence Bureau, the British intelligence bureau called the MI5 is founded.

1910

American murderer Dr. Hawley Crippen (1862–1910) is captured while on the lam, after a ship's captain spots the disguised doctor among his passengers and sends a message to the press and police via the newly invented radio.

c. 1910

Frenchman Edmund Locard proposes a concept known as "Locard's Exchange Principle" which states that whenever a criminal comes into contact with a victim, object, or a crime scene, he or she will leave behind (and take away) evidence.

1911

British archeologist Charles Dawson reveals the first of many fossil finds (including the remains of the so-called Piltdown Man) that are shown to be hoaxes in the 1950s.

1919

American swindler Charles Ponzi defrauds thousands of people with his promise to double the value of their original investments in just 90 days. Today, these financial scams are called Ponzi schemes.

1919

In baseball's World Series, eight players from the Chicago White Sox are accused of "fixing" the Series to give the championship to the Cincinnati Reds. The scandalous team is dubbed the "Black Sox" in the press.

1929

Throughout the 1920s, Chicago gangland legend Al Capone led a crime spree culminating in the St. Valentine's Day Massacre on February 14th, in which seven men are killed with 150 bullets.

1932

The child of American aviation legend Charles Lindbergh is kidnapped in a case that enraptured the nation; although the ransom is paid, the baby is killed. Two years later, FBI agents track down the murderer by tracing the ransom money.

1934

Police officers ambush and kill Bonnie Parker (b. 1910) and Clyde Barrow (b. 1909), an infamous pair of U.S. bank robbers.

Poster for Lindbergh baby

1934

The Federal Penitentiary at Alcatraz Island in the San Francisco Bay ("The Rock") opens its doors.

1947

The National Security Act establishes the Central Intelligence Agency (CIA) in the United States.

1950

The Israeli intelligence agency MOSSAD is founded.

1953

The infamous Russian Committee of State Security (KGB) is founded.

1958

The Service de Documentation Exterieure et Contre-Espionage (SDECE) is created in France; in 1982, it is replaced with the DGSE.

1960s

The first computer hackers emerge, predominantly at MIT in Boston, MA. The word "hack" was used at MIT to describe a particularly inspired prank.

1963

In the Great Train Robbery, Britain's most famous theft, a gang of thieves steals used banknotes from mailbags carried on a train.

1974

Patty Hearst, granddaughter of a legendary newspaper publisher, is kidnapped; two months later, she appears in a bank robbery video brandishing a gun. Hearst is later arrested and sent to prison for her crime, despite her lawyers claim that she was brainwashed at the time.

1984

DNA evidence becomes the universal standard for identification, ultimately changing the face of detective work.

1992

John Gotti, the head of a major crime family in New York City, is charged with racketeering and sentenced to life in prison without parole.

1994

Phoolan Devi, better known as India's "Bandit Queen" is released from prison, becoming a folk hero.

1995

In a trial that created a media sensation around the world, former American professional football player O.J. Simpson is found not guilty of murder.

1998

U.S. math professor-turned-mail-bomber Theodore Kaczynski ("The Unabomber") pleads guilty.

2004

In a high profile case that gripped the media, Californian Scott Peterson is found guilty of killing his wife and unborn child. In 2005, Peterson is sentenced to die for his crime.

Ted Kaczynski ("The Unabomber")

Find out more

Badge from French
National Shooting Center

WHILE FOLLOWING A LIFE OF CRIME is
not recommended, there are several legal
ways that you can find out more about
crime, criminals, and detective
work. For an insider's look at
crimefighting, call your local
law enforcement community
outreach program, and arrange for a police
officer or detective to visit your school.
Watching court coverage or crime dramas
on TV can bring you up-to-date with
the latest in criminal justice.

Hat worn by London police

"Mountie" jacket with holster

Police memorabilia

Police whistle

VISIT A POLICE MUSEUM
What do law enforcement
agencies do with all those
things they confiscate? Some
of the items end up in police
department museums. You won't get
into the oldest and most notorious of these
exhibits—Scotland Yard's "Black Museum"
in London, England—unless you are a police
officer. But many city police departments allow
the public to visit their collections of memorabilia
related to the police force. Check the box on the
right or the Internet for details.

MEET A POLICE OFFICER
Do you want to find out
about law enforcement
in your own community?
Contact the community
outreach department
of your local police
department, and arrange
for an officer to visit your
school to discuss crime
prevention and careers
in law enforcement.

USEFUL WEB SITES

www.ojp.usdoj.gov/bjs/
The latest in crime statistics from the Department of Justice

www.fbi.gov
The Internet home of the Federal Bureau of Investigation

www.ncpc.org
Home page of the National Crime Prevention Council

www.mcgruff.org
McGruff the Crime Dog hosts this fun site for kids

GO BEHIND BARS
If you are planning a trip to San
Francisco, consider a visit to the
former federal penitentiary at
Alcatraz Island. A National
Park Service guide can lead you
on a fascinating tour, or take
the audio tour, which brings the
empty cells alive with the
stories of former guards and
prisoners and the sounds you
might hear as a new convict
when you approached your cell
for the first time. In some states,
operational prisons offer tours
to school groups. Check the
Internet for details.

VISIT A COURTROOM
Courts belong to the public, and are open for visits when court is not in session. To find out about visiting a courthouse in your county, ask your parents or teacher to contact the Trial Court Administrator at your county courthouse. There may be age restrictions or other regulations. The administrator should also be able to tell you how to arrange a visit to a court of appeals in your area.

CRIME ON TELEVISION
Television crime dramas work directly with police consultants to make sure the shows give an accurate picture of detective work and the forensic sciences. There are a number of excellent shows on the air that will keep you up-to-date with the latest crime-fighting advances (while keeping you on the edge of your seat).

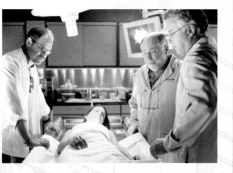

Places to Visit

FEDERAL BUREAU OF INVESTIGATIONS HEADQUARTERS, WASHINGTON, D.C.
Expected to reopen after renovations in 2007, this popular tour will review some of the FBI's greatest cases and investigations.

SUPREME COURT, WASHINGTON, D.C.
Visit the highest court in the land. When the court is in session, you may be able to observe for a few minutes.

TEXAS RANGER HALL OF FAME AND MUSEUM, WACO, TX
The official historical center of the legendary Texas Rangers

SEATTLE METROPOLITAN POLICE MUSEUM, SEATTLE, WA
Discover the history of law enforcement in the American Northwest.

PHOENIX POLICE MUSEUM, PHOENIX, AZ
This museum features a recreation of an early 1900s police station.

CLEVELAND POLICE AND HISTORICAL SOCIETY MUSEUM, CLEVELAND, OH
Discover the history of Cleveland's police force with a visit to this museum

ROYAL CANADIAN MOUNTED POLICE CENTENNIAL MUSEUM, REGINA, SASKATCHEWAN
Dedicated to more than 125 years of service of the "Mounties"

VISIT THE FBI
It is far better to visit the FBI than for the FBI to visit you. Renovations at FBI headquarters in Washington, D.C., have closed its popular public tour, which featured a stop on a real firing range. But when the tour reopens in the early part of 2007, it is sure to be as popular as ever. Check the official FBI Web site for the latest news.

Glossary

AMPEL PROBE A tool used to inspect evidence without the risk of contamination or exposure. An ampel probe works like an extension of the human hand.

ANTHROPOMETRY An identification system based on the measurement of body parts. Developed in 1892, it was the first scientific system used to identify criminals.

ARSON The crime of voluntarily setting a building on fire for an unjust reason; for example, burning one's own home in order to collect insurance money

ASSASSIN Someone who sets out to kill another individual. Assassins especially target prominent public figures.

AUTOPSY The examination of a cadaver, or dead bod in an attempt to identify its cause of death.

BAIL Money given to a court as security when a person accused of a crime is released from jail. Bail is forfeited if the accused fails to appear.

BALLISTICS The study of how weapons function

Body armor

BODY ARMOR Armor that entirely protects the person wearing it. Someone is likely to wear body armor when entering a dangerous situation.

BOOTLEG To produce, distribute, and sell something without receiving permission; also, an item sold in this way. People often create bootleg copies of videos or CDs.

BOUNTY HUNTER A person that searches for a criminal or fugitive for the purpose of obtaining the reward money.

BURGLARY The act of entering a building with the intention of stealing or committing a crime.

CENTRIFUGE A machine or device that spins a container very quickly, leading to the separation of liquids and solids through centrifugal action; often used in forensics

COMMON LAW A legal system based on decisions made in a courtroom rather than decisions made by the legislative branch of government

CONVICT A person who has been found guilty of committing a crime

COUNTERFEIT A false copy or replica of something genuine

CRIME SCENE The location where a crime was committed. Crime scenes are usually closed off so that police may search the area for evidence.

CRIME WAVE A sudden increase in the number of recorded crimes

DEFENSE Something that gives protection against danger

DENTAL INDENTIFICATION The practice of inspecting people's teeth after their death in order to help identify them. This system is precise because no two people have identical dental histories.

DETECTIVE Someone who investigates crimes, either as part of a government agency or on a freelance basis

Centrifuge

DNA EVIDENCE Evidence based on DNA, the unique genetic coding found in our cells. Usually, DNA found at a crime scene (in blood or tissue, for example) is compared with DNA taken from a suspect in order to prove their involvement.

EVIDENCE Something that points towards a specific idea or conclusion

EXPLOSIVES A chemical substance that has the ability to create an explosion. Explosives are often used as weapons or a means to cause harm.

EXTORTION The practice of illegally obtaining something, usually money, through force or intimidation

FINGERPRINT ANALYSIS The investigation or breakdown of the unique set of ridges on the tip of a finger, also known as a fingerprint

FIX To establish something as definite. Also, to influence the result of an event (a horse race or an election, for example) to one's advantage by bribery, trickery, etc.

FORENSIC SCIENCE A branch of science dedicated to solving crimes by examining the evidence, using advanced technical procedures. A forensic examination can often explain how someone died.

FORGERY The act of reating an illegal duplicate of something in a deceptive manner. Common examples are forged signatures or documents.

Investigators work at a crime scene.

GANGSTER A member of a professional crime organization

HIGHWAYMAN A term used in the past to signify an armed man on a horse who stole from people traveling on public roads

HOSTAGE Someone who is taken prisoner by an armed individual in order to persuade others to adhere to the hostage-taker's commands and orders

JUSTICE The maintining of fairness and propriety, especially through laws

KIDNAPPING To forcefully take a person into possession, usually with the intention of requesting money in exchange for the person's release

LARCENY The act of stealing from another person without actually trespassing or invading anyone's property

LAW Rules and regulations enacted by society to maintain and establish order

LOOT To steal from stores and shops while violent or distracting events, such as a power outage or a riot, are occurring

MAFIA A criminal organization that originated in Sicily and continues to be active in Italy and the U.S. This close-knit group is notorious for going to violent extremes to protect its members.

MONEY LAUNDERING Anything done with the intent of hiding the source of illegally obtained money

NIGHT STICK A police baton used for hitting or restraining a criminal

ORGANIZED CRIME Crimes that are committed by members of criminal organizations or groups

PARDON An official act releasing someone from all penalties for a particular crime

PETTY THEFT The act of taking something insignificant or worthless that does not belong to you

PICKPOCKET A thief who robs or steals from purses, pockets, or wallets, often in a large crowd

PIRACY The illegal distribution of unauthorized intellectual property. This most often describes the theft of computer software, music, or movies.

POLICE LINEUP The process of arranging suspects in an organized row so that a victim may attempt to visually identify the guilty party

PROHIBITION The act of making something officially forbidden or illegal

PROSECUTE To bring someone to court and officially accuse them of being guilty of a particular crime

RANSOM An amount of money that is demanded by a criminal, particularly a kidnapper, in exchange for the release of someone who has been taken prisoner

RANSOM NOTE A note left by a criminal or kidnapper that lists what they are demanding in exchange for the release of a prisoner

REFRACTIVE INDEX A property of a material that determines how much light will bend when it passes into that material from another. The greater the difference in the refractive index of two materials, the more the light will bend.

SENTENCE To impose a specific punishment on someone who has been found guilty of a crime

SMUGGLE To secretly bring people or items to or from a place, in violation of the law

STATUTORY LAW A law that has been officially approved and recorded

STAKEOUT The ongoing surveillance of a particular place thought to be a center of criminal activity

STOCKS In the Middle Ages, a wooden frame enclosing one's hands, feet and, neck as a form of humiliating public punishment

SURVEILLANCE The act of k eeping a close eye on a person or location, often as part of a criminal investigation

SWINDLE To obtain something through deceitful and criminal action

TAX EVASION Any instance where someone attempts to illegally avoid paying taxes, usually through dishonest reporting

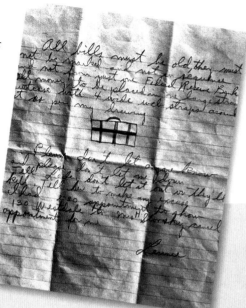

Ransom note

TELEPHONE TAP A common police and government method of listening in on a suspected criminal's phone conversation as part of an investigation

TERRORISM An act of violence or cruelty intended to intimidate a government into meeting certain political demands

ULTRAVIOLET LIGHT Light which has a wavelength that is beyond the color violet in the range of colors that are visible to human beings. Ultraviolet light, or UV, causes skin to grow darker in the sun.

Suspects in a police lineup

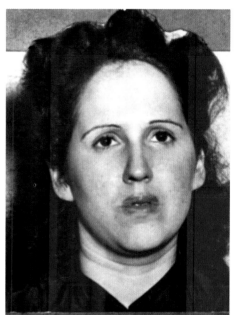  

 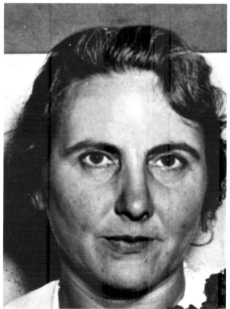 

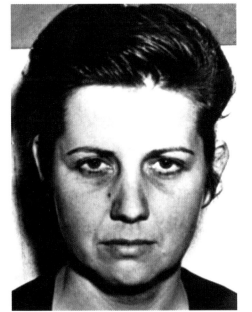
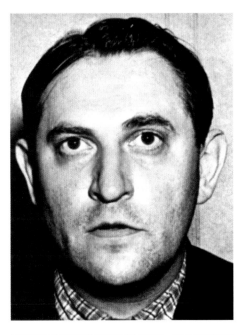
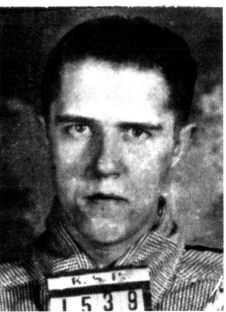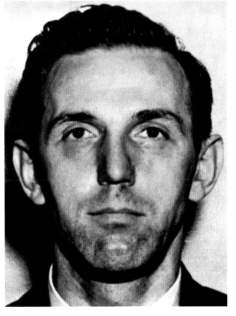

72-page Eyewitness Titles

American Revolution
Amphibian
Ancient China
Ancient Egypt
Ancient Greece
Ancient Rome
Arms & Armor
Astronomy
Aztec, Inca & Maya
Baseball
Basketball
Bird
Castle
Car
Cat
Chemistry
Crime & Detection
Crystal & Gem
Dance
Dinosaur
Dog
Early Humans
Earth
Ecology
Electricity
Explorer
Fish
Flying Machine
Food

Fossil
Future
Horse
Human Body
Hurricane & Tornado
Insect
Islam
Invention
Jungle
Knight
Mammal
Mars
Medieval Life
Money
Mummy
Music
Mythology
NASCAR
North American
  Indian
Ocean
Olympics
PhotographyPirate
Plant

Pond & River
Pyramid
Religion
Rocks & Minerals
Seashore
Shakespeare
Shark
Shipwreck
Skeleton
Soccer
Space
  Exploration
Sports
Titanic
Tree
Vietnam War
Viking
Volcano &
  Earthquake
Weather
Whale
Wild West
World War I
World War II

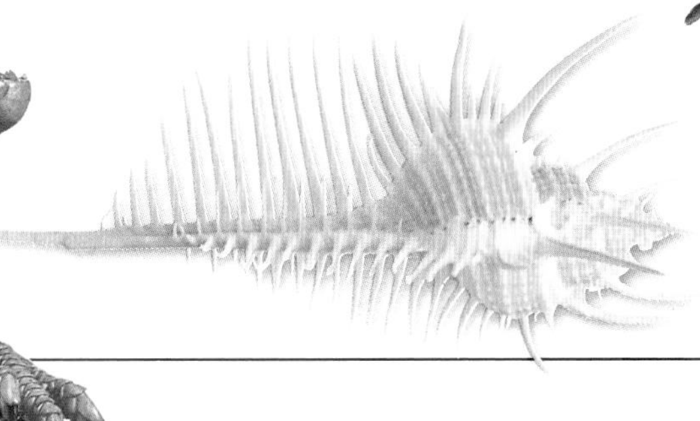

Other Eyewitness Titles

Africa
Archeology
Arctic & Antarctic
Battle
Bible Lands
Boat
Book
Buddhism
Building
Butterfly & Moth
Christianity
Civil War
Costume
Cowboy
Desert
Eagle & Birds of Prey
Electronics
Elephant
Energy
Epidemic
Everest
Evolution

Farm
Film
First Ladies
Flag
Football
Force & Motion
Gorilla
Goya
Impressionism
India
Judaism
Leonardo & His Times
Life
Light
Manet
Matter
Media & Communication
Medicine
Monet
Perspective
Prehistoric Life
Presidents

Renaissance
Reptile
Rescue
Robot
Russia
Shell
Spy
Submarine
Super Bowl
Technology
Texas
Time & Space
Train
Universe
Van Gogh
Watercolor
Witches & Magic Makers
World Series

Index

A B C

alarm system 16, 39
Alcatraz 13, 57; Birdman of 12, 13
alcohol trade, illegal 24, 28
analysis: chemical 46, 47; dust/soil 43, 46
animal trade, illegal 28
arson 30, 31, 47
assassination 58
badges 11, 32, 34
bail bonds/bondsman 15
ballistics 42, 43, 46
Bandit Queen, the 56
Barrows, the 57
Bertillon, Alphonse 50, 53
Billy's and Charley's 20
Billy the Kid 14
black market 8
blood 41, 42, 44, 47
Blood, Thomas 16
bodily fluids 46, 47
body armor 16, 34, 55, 57
"bog man" (Pete Marsh) 9
Boggs, J.S.G. 59
bombings 25, 27, 52, 54, 55
Bonaparte, Napoleon 46
Bonnie and Clyde 57
bounty hunter 14, 15
Bow Street Runner 10, 35
Brusca, Giovanni 27
Brussel, Dr. James 52
bugging device 38
bullet hole 42, 57
burglary 16, 17, 37, 43, 59
Byrnes, Thomas 50
Caesar, Gaius Julius 22
camera, concealed 38
Capone, Al 13, 24, 25
card trickster 18, 19
Cassidy, Butch 56; and the Sundance Kid 56
CCTV (closed circuit television) 38
Chandler, Raymond 37
Charles II, King 16
Chatterton, Thomas 20
Chicago gangsters 24, 25, 58
Confessore, Alphonse 19
Confucius 12
con men 18, 19
Costello, Frank 25
counterfeiting 20, 21
courts 12, 13, 15
criminal: mind 52; records 36, 50, 53; types 52
Crippen, Dr. 22
crowd control 34
custody 15
customs officer 28, 29, 54

D E F

Darwin, Charles 52
death sentence 12
dental identification 49
Department of Justice 24
DeSalvo, Albert ("the Boston Strangler") 52
detective 22, 36–39; female 37; "psychic" 37
detective agency 11
detective stories 36, 37, 39
Dew, Det. Insp. Walter 22
Dickens, Charles 8, 54
Dillinger, John 16, 17
DNA 22, 44–46; biological pattern 45; profiling 45
Draco 8
drugs 26, 28, 29, 37, 47, 54
Dupont 53
Eaton, Charley 20
electric chair 22
execution 8, 52, 56
explosives 54
extortion 26
facial reconstruction 48, 49
Farr, Sheriff Edward 13
FBI 15, 16, 22, 24, 58; Public Enemy list 16, 24
fibres, clothing 36, 40, 46
Fielding, Sir Henry 10
fingerprints 36, 40–42, 44, 45, 53; classification of 45; dusting 44, 45; genetic 44
fire investigation unit 30, 31; and equipment 30, 31
flying squad 55
forensic science 21, 30, 36, 37, 40, 42–44, 46, 47, 49, 50
forgery 20, 21, 59
Foster, Jodie 58

G H I

Gall, Dr. Franz 52
gallows 14, 16
Galton, Francis 44
gambling/betting 14, 18, 25–27; casinos 27; dens 26; roulette 27
gangs: motorcycle 50; Yakuza 26; Yamaguchi-gumi 26
Garrett, Sheriff Pat 14
garrotting 10
Gerasimov, Mikhail 48
Giancana, Sam 25
glass, broken 42, 43
Grant, Julius 21
Great Train Robbers 17, 57
Grigoriev, Prof. 48
gun running 26, 29
guns 10, 11, 13–17, 24, 25, 33, 35, 42, 46, 55–58
handcuffs/leg irons 13, 32
handwriting expert 43
hanging 12–13, 22, 58
Hauptmann, Bruno 22
Henry, Edward 45
Herschel, William 44
highwayman 14, 52, 56
Hinckley, John 58
Hirasawa 23
Hitler, Adolf 21; diaries 21
Hoover, John Edgar 24
Hory, Elmyr de 21
hostage taking 35
ink and roll 44
insurance claims 18, 31, 59
Interpol 36

J K L M

James, Frank 11
James, Jesse 11–13
Jeffreys, Alec 45
Judicial Identification Service 53
Justinian the Great 8
Kefauver, Senator 25
Kelly, Machine Gun 13
Kelly, Ned 16
Kennedy, John F. 58
Kerner, Annette 37
Ketchum, Black Jack 13
kidnapping 22, 23
Landru, Henri-Desiré 23
La Reynie 10
laser reconstruction 49
Lauvergne 52
laws: Chinese 12; common 10; Draconian 8; religious 8; Roman 8, 9; tribal 9; written/statute 10
Legros, Fernand 21
Le Neve, Ethel 22
Leopold, Nathan 23
Lincoln, Abraham 11
Lindbergh, Charles 22
Lindow Man 9; Woman 58
line-up 50
Listiev, Vladislav 27
Locard, Edmond 40
lockpicks 37
Loeb, Richard 23
Lombroso, Cesare 52
loot/looters 8, 17, 24
Louvois 10
Lucan, "Lucky" 23
lynching 12
Mafia 25–27
Mandrin, Louis 56
manhunts 27
marksmen 35
Metesky, George ("the Mad Bomber") 52
Metropolitan Police (London) 10, 11, 35, 50, 54
microcentrifuge 47
microscopes 46, 43
Midas, King 49
money-laundering 26
money lending 26
Morgan, Henry 58
Morton, Samuel "Nails" 58
mugging 16
"mug shots" 50, 53
Müller, Dr. 31
murder 9, 13, 14, 22–25, 31, 40, 46, 47, 49, 55–58
Murelli, Sister Alvina 26

N O P R

Neave, Richard 48, 49
Ness, Eliot 24; and "the Untouchables" 24
Niedersachsen 32
organized crime 24–27, 33
Oswald, Lee Harvey 58
outlaw/bandit 11–13, 52, 56
pardons: free 14; royal 16
Parker, George C. 19
pathologist 40, 47, 49
Peace, Charlie 18
peat bogs 9, 58
Peel, Sir Robert 10
peelers/bobbies 10, 32
Penry, Jacques 51
Photo-fit (Penry Facial Identification Technique) 51
photographic evidence 37, 38, 40, 42, 44, 49–51, 53, 55
phrenology 52
PI (private investigator) 36, 37
pickpocket 8
Pinkerton, Allan 11, 37
Pinkerton's National Detective Agency 11
piracy 28, 29, 58
poisoning 22, 23, 46, 47; arsenic 20, 46; cyanide 23
police forces 8, 10, 11, 15, 16, 26–35, 38, 50; air transport 29, 54; dogs 54, 55; horses 35; mounted 10, 33, 35, 55; national 10, 11, 27, 32–36, 40, 50, 53; riot 26, 34; tipstaff 11; women/WPCs 33
Ponzi, Charles 19
postmortem 40, 47
Price, Karen 48, 49
prints: foot/tire 40, 42, 46
prison 9, 13, 16–19, 31, 52
Prohibition 24, 26
protective equipment 10, 15, 32–35, 55; rattle/whistle 10, 32; truncheon 10, 32, 33, 35; weapons 10
psychiatry/psychology 52
ram raiding 17
ransom demand 22, 23, 50
Reagan, Ronald 58
refractive index 43
revenge killing 31, 48
rewards 11, 15, 16
Rex III 55
robbers 11, 23, 31, 56–58; bank 11, 15, 16, 38, 56;
train 11, 13, 17, 56, 57
Roberts, Estelle 37
Robin Hood 26, 56
rubbish, clues in 43

S T U

safety deposit box 17
Scotland Yard 10, 22
searching for evidence 30, 31, 40–55
Secret Service 58
security officers 29
sheriffs 11, 14, 15
shoot-outs/sieges 13, 16, 35
skeletons/skulls 48, 49
Smith, Billy 20
smuggling 27–29, 54, 56
sniffer dogs 54, 55
SOCO 31, 40–42, 50
Spaggiari, Albert 59
spies 18
stabbing 9, 22
stakeout 39
strangulation 9
surveillance 36–39
swindles 18, 19, 52
Takenaka, Masahisa 26
tattoos 50
tax evasion 25
telephone tapping 38, 39
terrorism 29
theft 12, 16, 17, 29, 37, 39, 52, 53; petty larceny 12
thief takers 14
Thompson, Alvon C. 59
tool marks 43
Triads, Chinese 26, 50
Turpin, Dick 14, 56
uniforms 10, 11, 13, 32, 33

V W X

Vanezis, Dr. Peter 49
Viccei, Valerio 17
videofit, computer-aided 51
Vidocq 11
violent crimes 12, 16, 24–27
voiceprints 50
wanted posters 16, 17, 57
Warren, Sir Charles 54
Wild West 11–15, 56
witnesses 36, 50, 51
x-ray surveillance 29

Acknowledgments

The publisher would like to thank:
David Roberts; Ross Simms and the Winchcombe Folk and Police Museum; Sam Tree of Keygrove Marketing Ltd.; Assistant Divisional Officer Derek Thorpe and the Fire Investigation Unit at Acton Police Station; Rentokil Pest Control; Dr. Brian Widdop of the Medical Toxicology Unit Laboratory; Shona Lowe of HM Customs and Excise; The Metropolitan Police Museum; Mike Wombwell; the Commissioner for the City of London Police for his kind permission to photograph Penry's Photo-fit kit; Bill Harriman of JWF Harriman
Researcher: Robert Graham
Design and editorial coordinators: Vicky Wharton, Jayne Parsons, Miranda Smith
Design and editorial assistance: Goldberry Broad, Darren Troughton, Jake Williamson, Julie Ferris, Nancy Jones, Susila Baybars
Additional photography: Geoff Dann, Gary Ombler; Richard Shellabear
Photographic assistance: Gary Ombler, Andy Kamorovski
Index: Marion Dent

Picture Credits:
The publisher would like to thank the following for their kind permission to reproduce their photographs:
a=above; b=below; c=center; l=left; r=right; t=top
Action Plus: Glyn Kirk 18cl; **Archive Photos**: 19ca, 24tr; Lambert 19r; **Archive Photos France**: 21ca, 35tr; **J.S.G. Boggs**: 59tl; **The British Council**: Anita Corbin & John O'Grady 45clb; **The British Film Institute**: © Warner Bros. 56tr; **The British Museum**: 14tr, 20tr, 20cb, 20crb, 21cr; **Bruce Coleman Collection**: Luiz Claudio Marigo 28br; **Camera Press**: Lionel Cherruault 50cl; Dennis Stone 29tl; **Christies Images**: 22bc; **Corbis**: Bettmann 14bl, 14br, 37tr; Bettmann/UPI 24bl, 24br, 25tl, 25br, 52tr, 52cr; Everett 36bl; **Courtesy of Diners Club International**: 19c; **ET Archive**: British Museum 12tr; Tate Gallery 20br; **Mary Evans Picture Library**: 8tl, 10br, 11cl, 12tl, 13tl, 14cr, 14bc, 16bl, 19cb, 22tr, 22cl, 24cl, 28cl, 28bl, 29br, 36tl, 44tc, 45tl, 46tl, 52bl, 52br, 53crb; Explorer 9tl; **Fortean Picture Library**: Dr. Elmar R. Gruber 9tr; **The Ronald Grant Archive**: © United Artists 37tl; © Warner Bros. 58bc; **Robert**

Harding Picture Library: 34bl; FPG International 31tl; **David Hoffman**: 29tc, 31cr, 45tr; **Hulton Getty**: 8cl, 8cra, 8bl, 11tl, 16tl, 16cr, 17tl, 17tr, 18tr, 23tl, 23tc, 23tr, 23cl, 23cra, 33br, 53tl, 56cl; **The Image Bank**: Barros & Barros 40tr; **The Kobal Collection**: © Touchstone Pictures 39cra; © 20th Century Fox 50tr, 56br; **H. Keith Melton**: 37c; **Metropolitan Police Service**: 34br, 35c, 54cl, 55tl; **Microscopix**: Andrew Syred 46cll, 46cl, 46c; **Moviestore Collection**: © United Artists 15cl; **News International Associated Services**: 21br, 23crb; **Rex Features**: 42crb, 54bl, 59c; Hugh Routledge & Peter Bennett 51tl; Nils Jorgensen 43bc; Julian Makey 55cra, 55br; James Morgan 55c; John Shelley 35bl; Sipa/Dieter Ludwig 56bl; The Times 35tl; Today 46bc, 47cr; **Science Photo Library**: 49br; American Science and Engineering 29tr; Klaus Guldbrandsen 45bl; Peter Menzel 40clb, 46tr; Hank Morgan 50cr; **Service de l'Information et des Relations Publiques**: Tanguy Delamotte 34tr; **Frank Spooner Pictures**: 59tr; Gamma/G. Bassignac 41br; Georges Merillon 54 clb; Olivier Pighetti 15tl, 15tr; Olympia/Palazzotto 27tl; **Sygma**: Rufo 27cr; Sion Touhig 55tr; **Telegraph Colour Library**: 30tl; Ron Chapple 44bl; Colorific/Tim Graham 33brr, 34cl; **Topham**

Picturepoint: 12bl, 12cr, 37tc, 37bl, 48tr, 58bl, 58cl, 58cr; Associated Press 25bl, 26bl, 26br, 27tr, 26tr; Press Association 49tl; **Roger-Viollet**: 8br, 36br; **Jerry Young**: 48cll, 48cl, 48cr, 48br, 49tr, 49c, 49cr.

Corbis: 68-69; Archivo Iconografico, S.A. 66tl; Bettmann 66c, 67cr, 67tl; Fat Chance Productions 67br; Neal Preston 68-69bc; Paul A. Souders 66tr; William Whitehurst 66-67
Getty Images: 66cl; The Image Bank 64c; Time Life Pictures 67tr
PictureQuest: Table Mesa Prod. 68bl
Science Photo Library/Photo Researchers: 64bl, 65cl, 65tc
Courtesy of the Sherlock Holmes Museum, London: 64tl

Jacket images: *Front*: DK Images: Andy Crawford/Courtesy of Sam Tree at Keygrove Marketing Ltd (tr); Andy Crawford/ David Roberts (cal); Andy Crawford/Ross Simms and the Winchcombe Folk and Police Museum (cb, cfr, cla); Science Photo Library: Dr. Jeremy Burgess (b). *Back*: DK Images: Andy Crawford/David Roberts (bl); Andy Crawford/Ross Simms and the Winchcombe Folk and Police Museum (cb, cfr, cla); Geoff Dann/Commissioner for the City of London Police (cfl).